Watering the
Greyhound Garden

Watering the Greyhound Garden

Stories from the Streets of San Francisco

Warren B. Smith

MOUNTAIN STREAM PRESS

Watering the Greyhound Garden
Copyright © 2013 by Warren B. Smith
First Edition

Mountain Stream Press
P.O. Box 1794
Magalia, CA 95954

greyhoundgarden@gmail.com

Cover design by Letizia Albamonte.

Excerpts from the *San Francisco Chronicle* on pages 56-58, 170, and 173-174. *San Francisco Chronicle*/copyright.com. Used by permission.

Photo on page 52 by John O'Neill. Used by permission.

Photo on page 74 by Gloria Judd. Used by permission.

Photo on page 82 from the *San Francisco Chronicle*. ©Stephanie Maze/*San Francisco Chronicle*/Corbis. Used by permission.

Photos on pages x and 98 from the *San Francisco Chronicle*. ©John O'Hara/*San Francisco Chronicle*/Corbis. Used by permission.

Photos on pages 4 and 178 from the San Francisco History Center, San Francisco Public Library. Used by permission.

LIKE A ROLLING STONE ©1965 by Warner Bros. Inc.; renewed 1993 by Special Rider Music. All rights reserved. International copyright secured. Reprinted by permission.

THE GAMBLER ©1978 Sony/ATV Music Publishing LLC. All rights administered by Sony/ATV Music Publishing LLC, 8 Music Square West, Nashville, TN 37203. All rights reserved. Used by permission.

CALIFORNIA, HERE I COME (Public domain).

DO-RE-MI ©1940 Sony/ATV Music Publishing LLC. All rights administered by Sony/ATV Music Publishing LLC, 8 Music Square West, Nashville, TN 37203. All rights reserved. Used by permission.

PICK A BALE OF COTTON (Public domain).

GOD REST YE MERRY GENTLEMEN (Public domain).

FOREVER YOUNG ©1973 by Ram's Horn Music; renewed 2001 by Ram's Horn Music. All rights reserved. International copyright secured. Reprinted by permission.

Scripture quotations are taken from the *King James Version*.

To order additional copies of this book, call (800)247-6553.

ISBN: 978-0-9846461-2-8

Library of Congress Control Number: 2012944128

Printed in Canada

Dedication

To Travelers Aid International, formed in the mid-1800s when an inspired local citizenry in St. Louis, Missouri provided organized assistance to American pioneers and immigrants who were heading out West to seek their fortunes. Today, Travelers Aid continues to assist travelers with offices and outreach services across the United States, Puerto Rico, Canada, and Australia.

At a crucial time in my life, a volunteer position with San Francisco Travelers Aid inspired me to pursue a degree in social work. After I completed graduate school, that same San Francisco Travelers Aid hired me as one of their full-time social workers. I will always be grateful to Travelers Aid for the special work they do and for the deep impact they had in my life.

Contents

Acknowledgments

Special thanks to Chris Schleuss.

And many thanks to everyone who provided me with their own special brand of "travelers aid" at key times in my own journey through life—Warren and Betty Smith, Bobby Steel, Robert Steel, Brett Bachman, Bob Smith, Harry Sewall, Hayden and Arlene Evans, Luis Martorell, Ty Bartel, Cheryl Ford, Dave and Carol Winslow, Dana and Katie Anderson, Bill Carlson, Johanna Michaelsen, Pat McCue, Cheryl Marchal, Pat and Helene Sweeney, my beloved wife Joy, and most especially—God.

I want to express my heartfelt gratitude to everyone at the San Francisco Travelers Aid Society—Arlin Alger, Carol Bohnsack, Barbara Glesner, Cate Maloney, Marjorie Montelius, Debbie Whitehouse, Dawn, Ginny, Irene, Jackie, and all the other employees and volunteers I worked with.

Thanks also to Billie at FROC for her encouragement and early typing of these stories; Letizia Albamonte for her cover; Gene Nicolelli at the Greyhound Museum in Hibbing, Minnesota and former Greyhound ticket agent Jack Brunelle for answering my many questions; Richard Geiger, Gary Fong, Elly Oxman, and Rick Romagosa at the *San Francisco Chronicle* and photo curator Christina Moretta at the San Francisco Public Library for helping me to obtain necessary photographs; and Tom Clark, Superintendent of Canyon de Chelly National Monument for his assistance.

And last but not least, thanks to Joy Smith, Bill Carlson, Stephen Poole, Sarah Leslie, and Alison Smith for their editorial help; and to Betty Smith, Heather Powers, Maureen Valdivia, Carol Bohnsack, Kathy Wolfs Stewart, Vernon Rousseau, and Arlene Evans for their suggestions and various contributions.

My one regret is that my mother, Betty Smith, didn't live to see the publication of this book. She so loved hearing these Greyhound stories.

Warren Smith at the Travelers Aid booth
(Photo by John O'Hara)

Note to the Reader

All the stories in this book are true. They took place when I was employed as the After-Hours Social Worker for the San Francisco Travelers Aid Society from 1976-1978. Prior to my deep involvement in New Age/New Spirituality and my later conversion to the Christian faith, I was paid to be a "Good Samaritan" at the San Francisco Greyhound Bus Terminal. It was an amazing first job for a fledgling social worker. Fresh out of graduate school, I was at times overeager and unorthodox in my methods as I always took a hands-on approach in working with people. But I loved my job and I loved the people I was trying to help.

The San Francisco Travelers Aid Society was established in 1914. Our mission at Travelers Aid was to meet the special needs of travelers who had recently arrived in the city and were experiencing problems of almost every imaginable type. Funded primarily by the people of San Francisco through United Way, Travelers Aid provided troubled travelers with short-term housing, food, crisis counseling, transportation, community referrals—whatever was necessary to get them back on their feet and moving again.

While our main office at 38 Mason Street was open nine-to-five Monday through Friday, we also had outreach booths at the Greyhound bus station and the San Francisco International Airport. I worked primarily out of the Greyhound Tuesday through Friday evenings and all day Saturday.

Several years after leaving Travelers Aid, I began writing about my experiences with the agency. With pages of personal notes and many stories fresh in mind, I wrote as much as I could in my spare time. However, in 1983 at the height of my writing, certain events in my life forced me to put the book aside. Over the ensuing years I wrote several other books—but I never got back to this one.

Then, in August of 2005, I found myself helping a childhood friend as he tried to escape New Orleans after Hurricane Katrina. The next month I assisted another friend who was driven from her Port Neches, Texas home during Hurricane Rita. As I worked with each of them and contacted numerous agencies and organizations to help them relocate, I recalled my job with Travelers Aid—I also remembered my unfinished book.

Reading through it, I was surprised at how much had been written and how easily I could move back into it. In those instances where minor details were still needed, I could fill them in to the best of my recollection. And while the conversations recorded weren't always verbatim accounts, I knew they were wholly consistent with what was said at the time. Thus, with much of the book written, I decided to finish what I had begun so many years previous.

Working around other writing projects and obligations, I finally completed the manuscript in the fall of 2012. All client names have been changed to maintain confidentiality; the names Kari, Anne, and Jan were used to protect the confidentiality of three non-clients. All geographical locations are accurate according to my original notes and to the best of my remembrance. However, the names of two small towns were changed to Carbon Glow and Holly Hill to further ensure client anonymity.

It should be noted that the stories in this book took place in the context of a particularly turbulent decade in the history of the San Francisco Bay Area—the 1970s. It was the post-Haight-Ashbury decade that witnessed the Symbionese Liberation Army (SLA) kidnapping of Patty Hearst; the attempted assassination of President Gerald Ford near Union Square; the actual assassinations of Mayor George Moscone and Supervisor Harvey Milk in their city hall offices; and the arrival of the infamous "Reverend" Jim Jones and the establishment of his People's Temple. It was also the decade when the "Zodiac" and "Zebra" murderers weren't the only killers loose on the streets of San Francisco. In the late 1970s, the AIDS virus was already percolating under the surface and would soon strike terror into the local gay community and the world at large.

Framed in what has been described as one of the most extraordinary decades in San Francisco history, I believe these stories are as relevant today as they were during that remarkable time.

–Warren Smith

City of San Francisco as seen through the Golden Gate Bridge

Prologue

Every day, countless travelers stream into the city of San Francisco. They come on planes and trains and midnight buses. They drive and they hitchhike. From the Gold Rush to the days of Haight-Ashbury, from the 1906 earthquake to the present day, the city has always been regarded as a place where you can start your life again. Its charm and mystique hold the promise of mystery and romance. This unique and beautiful city stirs the imagination and seems to beckon with what's missing in people's lives. And like a beacon by the Bay, it attracts lost and searching souls.

Many of these San Francisco newcomers arrive in trouble. Out of money and out of luck, they find themselves in crisis and need help fast. Dream trips become disasters as poor planning, unrealistic expectations, and unfortunate circumstances quickly turn their magic into misery. In the past, some of these newcomers ended up at the Greyhound bus station. Here they sat and worried and tried to figure out what to do next—about a job, a meal, and a place to stay. Survival became a way of life as they attempted to make it from day to day. The inner city became their world, the Greyhound depot their refuge and last resort.

The bus station was located downtown at Seventh and Mission. Because the Greyhound was where so many people had questions, problems, or found themselves stranded, the San Francisco Travelers Aid Society established an outreach booth right in the Greyhound lobby. As the After-Hours Social Worker for Travelers Aid working mainly out of the bus station, I covered the poor inner-city area known as the "Tenderloin." It was my job to help piece together the broken dreams and shattered travel plans of the people I saw—to encourage them and assist them in any way I could.

The Greyhound was a colorful, ragtag patchwork of people and problems, where the world seemed to meet itself in some strange kaleidoscopic way. Hustle and bustle met desperation and despair face to face. People going somewhere crossed paths with people going nowhere. More than just a depot for travelers on the go, the Greyhound was where people in crisis were suddenly forced to deal with their interrupted plans and faltering lives.

During my time with Travelers Aid, I came to understand that the Greyhound Bus Terminal was symbolic of the place where, sooner or later, we all get stuck in our own life journeys. When nothing seems to work and there's so little left to lose, we reach out for help—and mysteriously get it. Because our Travelers Aid booth was strategically located in the lobby of the bus station, we often had the privilege of providing that necessary help.

But perhaps the most important thing I learned while working at Travelers Aid was that whatever encouragement I provided to others through my job, I received back a hundredfold from the people we served. It is a simple fact of life that in truly giving we truly receive, and Travelers Aid was as much a godsend for me as it was for our clients. Being able to provide assistance to someone in need is a most amazing and wonderful thing. The following stories are about some of the people I met and worked with at the Greyhound bus station and on the streets of San Francisco.

…and he that watereth shall be watered also himself.

—Proverbs 11:25

Sign at the San Francisco Greyhound Bus Terminal

Walking to Work

...walk worthy of the vocation wherewith ye are called...
—Ephesians 4:1

The San Francisco Travelers Aid main office and our outreach booth at the Greyhound Bus Terminal were both located in a downtown part of the city known as the Tenderloin. While the Tenderloin borders the theater district on the north and ironically includes the Hilton Hotel, it is best defined by what singer Hank Williams described as "life's other side." Bars, liquor stores, cheap hotels, budget restaurants, porn shops, X-rated theaters, and massage parlors were scattered throughout the area. Panhandlers, drunks, drug addicts, prostitutes, the mentally ill, and the homeless sometimes seemed to be everywhere. Low-income seniors, struggling artists, college students, the working poor, and various ethnic groups formed a less-obvious backdrop to this unique urban melting pot known as the Tenderloin. St. Anthony's Dining Hall, the Tenderloin Clinic, Salvation Army, Hospitality House, Glide Memorial Church, and many other church and social service organizations were purposefully located in the Tenderloin neighborhood.

There are many stories about how the Tenderloin got its name. *Webster's New World Dictionary* defines the term as "any urban district similar to the Tenderloin—a former district in New York City, in which there was much graft and corruption." The Tenderloin name is also said to make reference to the many prostitutes who have always lived and worked in the area.

Although our main office was only three blocks from skid row, we were just around the corner from the San Francisco Visitors

Center and the famous cable car turn-around at Powell and
Market Streets. Located one block north of Market—the city's
main thoroughfare for downtown traffic—we were directly above
Polo's Italian Restaurant. Across the street going north to south
was a colorful fruit and vegetable market, the low-rent Ambassador
Hotel, a parking garage, Mike's hole-in-the-wall Athens Greek
Restaurant, and Sam's Hofbrau down on the corner of Market.
On our side of the street was the Moler Barber College and the
Bristol Hotel.

During the week, I began my workday in the early afternoon
at the main office. My quiet back office gave me a chance to see
clients in a more private setting than the busy Greyhound lobby
and allowed me to network with our day staff before heading
down to the bus station. On Wednesdays we closed our doors an
hour or two for our weekly staff meeting. Here we would discuss
difficult cases, share resources, have occasional guest speakers, and
mutually encourage one another. It was a welcome time-out from
our otherwise hectic week of seeing clients.

While some staff came and went, a core group was present
throughout my time with the agency—Marjorie, our always
proper, somewhat reserved director; Cate, our kind, supportive
social work supervisor; Carol, the personable, upbeat, thoroughly
professional social worker; and Arlin, the thoughtful and witty
social worker whose meticulous case notes were something to
behold. When I was a Travelers Aid volunteer in the early 1970s,
Arlin was the After-Hours Social Worker who supervised me
at the bus station. Through his handling of difficult cases, he
demonstrated what it meant to be non-judgmental—to meet
people right where they were at and really help them. When I
returned from graduate school, he had moved to the day program
at the main office and I was eventually hired to take his after-
hours position at the Greyhound. Other staff included Barbara,
our volunteer coordinator; Irene, the Director of our Tenderloin
Childcare Center (TLC); Jackie, our accountant; Ginny, another
social worker; and our three successive receptionists, Dawn,
Michael, and Debbie. It was a pleasure working with all of them.

It was always an interesting three-block walk along Market Street from our office to the Greyhound. Buses, cars, taxi cabs, trolley cars, and bicycles traveled up and down the broad thoroughfare as street people huddled in small groups, smoking *whatever* and listening to their ghetto blasters. Tourists with backpacks scurried past the many fast-food restaurants, discount movie theaters, and amusement arcades. Meanwhile street musicians—good and bad—played for the never-ending parade of passers-by as periodic panhandlers made their appeal for people's spare change.

On any given day, a bag lady shuffles along the sidewalk with her teeming shopping cart; an angry cab driver blasts his horn at a clueless jaywalker; a drunk is passed out in front of the Palace pool hall; an old woman feeds pigeons by the cut-rate camera store; the fresh aroma of clam chowder wafts out from the Palm Garden Grill; a pair of sneakers dangle from an overhead electrical line; and a voice was always calling out from some darkened doorway—"Hey, man, wanna buy some grass?"

Crossing the street at Jack-in-the-Box and turning left on Seventh, I walk by Esquire Photos, the Odd Fellows Building, Lyle Tuttle's Tattoo Museum, Travelers Liquors, and George's "read all about it" newsstand with the latest race results from the Bay Meadows Racetrack. Just past George's I arrive at the bus station.

Founded in the heart of Midwest iron ore country, the Greyhound Bus Lines was born in Hibbing, Minnesota— hometown of Bob Dylan—where, today, Greyhound Boulevard runs just northwest of Bob Dylan Drive. Dylan's song "Like a Rolling Stone" was like a Greyhound anthem as it described so many of the homeless and stranded people we saw at our Travelers Aid booth:

> *How does it feel*
> *To be on your own*
> *With no direction home*
> *Like a complete unknown*
> *Like a rolling stone?*

Suspended in time and space over the depot doorway at the base of the huge blue perpendicular sign was the famed Greyhound dog—the fastest dog on the face of the earth—going nowhere fast. The only dog mentioned by name in the Bible, standing guard over all the saints and sinners entering the depot. And what a remarkable group of saints and sinners they were! When Shakespeare wrote "All the world's a stage," he *must* have been sitting in the San Francisco Greyhound bus station. The dramas that unfolded there on a daily basis make today's reality TV shows pale in comparison. Just as Shakespeare's plays included a memorable cast of characters, the Greyhound bus station had its colorful characters too—people like Banjo Bobby Brown.

The Yountville Veteran

Wine is a mocker, strong drink is raging…
—Proverbs 20:1

"My name is Banjo Bobby Brown and I want five dollars—RIGHT NOW!"

The drunken man standing in front of me looked like Hollywood actor Robert Mitchum at the tail end of a long bender. His shirt was unbuttoned, revealing a bottle of whiskey stuffed down the front of his pants, and he was sweating profusely. A strange artificial vine twisted up and around the cane he was leaning on.

"Five bucks or I'll blow the place up!" he shouted.

He was demanding the money so he could buy a ticket to Yountville and the California Veterans Home where he claimed to be living. The facility was located in the beautiful Napa Valley wine country an hour or so north of San Francisco. I told Banjo Bobby that if he calmed down I would try to help—but first I needed to confirm that he really was a resident at the Veterans Home.

"Go ahead, call the SOBs," he barked defiantly. "I don't care!" With his words still ringing in the air, he broke into raucous laughter and embarked on a rooster-like strut around the Greyhound lobby. People shifted anxiously in their chairs. Banjo Bobby Brown had everyone's attention—and he was obviously enjoying it.

But there was a major problem in getting Banjo Bobby back to Yountville—there was no way Greyhound would let him travel on one of their buses in his clearly drunken state. Hoping to avoid a full-blown incident that would surely involve Greyhound security and most likely the police, I phoned the Yountville Veterans Home. It was a shot in the dark, but if Banjo Bobby lived there, maybe *they* could pick him up and transport him back to Yountville.

The clerk who answered the phone confirmed that while Bobby *did* live at the Veterans Home, he was officially AWOL— and extremely volatile when he was drunk and off his medication. He told me that for the last three days Banjo Bobby had been calling in bomb threats to their Yountville facility. However, the worker did have some encouraging news. If Travelers Aid could get Bobby over to the Veterans Hospital, the VA staff would drive him to Yountville once he was sober and back on his meds. But he advised me to call the police if Bobby refused to go to the hospital or became any more belligerent. After our conversation, I called the VA Hospital and they agreed to take responsibility for Bobby *if* I could somehow get him over to their emergency room.

Banjo Bobby was still parading around the lobby as I hung up the phone—yet he came right to our booth when I called his name. I explained how someone from the Veterans Hospital would take him to Yountville, but he had to get to the hospital for that to happen. I told him Travelers Aid would pay for a taxi if he promised to behave himself. After he grudgingly agreed, I led him out to one of the waiting cabs in front of the bus station. Leaning into the taxi, I described Banjo Bobby's situation to the driver and warned that his potential fare might be a handful. As fate would have it, the cabbie was a sympathetic veteran and more than willing to help. After getting Bobby into the cab and handing the obliging driver the fare and tip, I watched in relief as they drove off to the VA Hospital.

Back inside the Greyhound, I phoned the hospital to let them know that Banjo Bobby Brown was on his way. As I hung up the phone I noticed that the tension in the lobby had waned and several people were smiling at me and shaking their heads. They were probably thinking, "Thanks for getting that guy out of here *and* we wouldn't want your job for a million dollars!"

When I called the hospital an hour later to check on Bobby, it was a case of good news, bad news. I was told Banjo Bobby had arrived safely, but had been placed in restraints after attempting to "punch out" the intake nurse. When he sobered up, they would take him back to Yountville. The VA worker thanked me for getting Banjo Bobby off the streets and I thanked them for helping me to get him out of the bus station.

In retrospect, I probably should have called Greyhound security rather than a taxi for someone as unstable as Banjo Bobby Brown. At the very least I should have given the cab driver a bigger tip for taking on such a challenging passenger. But sometimes decisions have to be made quickly. Crisis was the name of the game at Travelers Aid, and on this Shakespearean stage known as the Greyhound bus station, it was "all's well that ends well" for people like Banjo Bobby Brown.

It was also "all's well that ends well" for a Sacramento woman who was fleeing an abusive husband who had tried to strangle her the night before.

La Casa Escapade

He that troubleth his own house shall inherit the wind...

—Proverbs 11:29

Early one afternoon I received a call from a Travelers Aid social worker in Sacramento. A woman named Marie was fleeing an abusive husband who tried to strangle her the night before. She would be arriving in San Francisco on a Greyhound bus in less than an hour. The social worker requested that I meet Marie's bus and immediately put her in a cab to Franklin Hospital. I was to then call La Casa de las Madres shelter for abused women; they would send one of their workers to pick up Marie at the hospital and take her to the shelter. I knew La Casa went to great lengths to protect the privacy of their address and wasn't surprised by the cloak-and-dagger transportation to and from Franklin Hospital. And—oh yes—there was one last piece of information the Sacramento worker told me—Marie's husband had discovered she was on the bus and was reportedly on his way to the San Francisco Greyhound.

After alerting Cate, my supervisor, I headed right over to the bus station. Knowing Marie's bus would be arriving shortly, I found the terminal manager and warned him there might be trouble. He immediately contacted Greyhound security. And though we were all now on full alert, none of us had any idea what Marie's husband looked like—or what he might do if he actually showed up.

I was waiting at the designated arrival gate when Marie's bus pulled in right on schedule. Very aware of Marie's situation, the driver introduced me to her as she stepped off the bus. The dark-haired woman in her late thirties was horrified when I told her that her husband was probably on his way to the bus station. I stressed the importance of leaving the depot as quickly as possible—how she would take a cab to Franklin Hospital and be transported from there to the women's shelter.

We were both a bit rattled as we waited for her luggage to be unloaded from the bus. But we soon discovered her bags weren't there. They were apparently on a second "section" bus that picked up the passenger overload in Sacramento. Although that bus would be arriving shortly, I urged Marie to leave the depot anyway—I'd retrieve her luggage and have someone from the shelter pick it up later. However, Marie would have nothing to do with it. She knew her husband was dangerous, but she refused to leave without her few remaining belongings. We would just pray that her luggage arrived before her husband.

Given her precarious situation, I rushed her over to the manager's office where she could remain secluded until her bags arrived. As we waited, her situation was feeling more and more like a scene from the television series "Streets of San Francisco," but the ace detectives played by Michael Douglas and Karl Malden were nowhere in sight. Thankfully, neither was Marie's husband—at least not yet.

Twenty minutes later, the delayed "sister" bus pulled into the depot. After grabbing Marie's luggage, we hurried through the lobby to a waiting cab. Firing quick instructions to the driver, I waved a hasty good-bye to Marie as they sped off to Franklin Hospital. My contact with her had been brief—only an hour or so—but its brevity was more than offset by its sheer intensity. As I walked back into the bus station, I was thankful there were places like La Casa de las Madres and I was also thankful this sort of thing didn't happen every day.

Marie had gambled that her luggage would show up before her husband. And while her gamble paid off, the Minnesota Gambler was not so fortunate.

The Minnesota Gambler

For the good that I would I do not:
but the evil which I would not, that I do.

—Romans 7:19

He looked like a Nordic sea captain as he stepped up to our Greyhound booth. Wearing a wide-brimmed black yachting cap, he had a squared-off gray beard with no mustache that made his jaw seem especially prominent. Jim was, in fact, of Scandinavian descent. The fifty-two-year-old man had been a machinist in a small town in Minnesota. For the last seventeen years he had run his own shop, but with their children grown, he and his wife decided to move to San Francisco to start a new life.

They left Minnesota with their life savings of $17,000 and a U-Haul trailer full of personal belongings. As they drove west, they took their time camping and sightseeing along the way. When they reached Reno, Nevada, Jim said he was ready for some "bright lights and a little blackjack." While his wife slept in a nearby motel room, he gambled away their entire nest egg—all $17,000—in less than six hours. She had their last fifty dollars that took them from Reno to San Francisco. They were staying with friends for now, but the future was very uncertain.

When Jim questioned me about work in the Bay Area, I was able to give him some definite hope; with his machinist skills he would probably have no trouble finding a job. After sharing information on employment opportunities and appropriate community resources, I asked him if he had ever thought about joining Gambler's Anonymous. He told me he had joined for a while but stopped attending years ago. With a forlorn look on his face, he said he wished he'd never dropped out, but that "Hindsight is always 20/20." After we finished talking, Jim thanked me for my time and we said good-bye. As he walked out of the Greyhound, the words to Kenny Rogers' song "The Gambler" ran through my mind:

> *You got to know when to hold 'em, know when to fold 'em*
> *Know when to walk away and know when to run.*

Hopefully, Jim *ran* to the next Gambler's Anonymous meeting and got his life back together. I still think of him whenever I hear that song.

The Minnesota Gambler and his wife would probably be happy *never* to return to Reno. It cost them nearly everything they owned. Paul, on the other hand, had everything he owned in Reno and needed to return at all costs.

"Reno"

Thou shalt love thy neighbor as thyself.
—Matthew 22:39

It was one of those wild and frantic Saturdays when it seemed as if the whole city was converging on the Greyhound bus station. Crowds of people flowed in and out of the depot. The darkened sidewalk in front of the terminal was littered with partially extinguished cigarette butts, and the smoke had a way of snaking its way up and hitting your nostrils when you least expected it. Inside the terminal it was much the same thing—it seemed that someone was always blowing smoke in your face.

Across Seventh Street, the Main Post Office was also busy. One of the few buildings to survive the 1906 earthquake, the historic building was a San Francisco landmark. Many of our Travelers Aid clients used general delivery at the post office for contact with family and social service agencies. It was where many of the homeless received their disability checks.

In the area in front of the Greyhound, where Jehovah's Witnesses, Hare Krishnas, and other groups often passed out their literature, the thin, elderly, black man stood in his usual spot. *"Help me Jesus. Help me Jesus. Help me Jesus,"* he beseechingly implored over and over and over again. But he wasn't sermonizing or passing out literature or asking for money. He was just doing what he was doing. It wouldn't have been Saturday at the Greyhound without him and I missed him when he wasn't there.

On the street, taxis were lined up to meet arriving passengers as several people checked the latest headlines at George's Newsstand. Inside the bus station, travelers sat patiently in the lobby as periodic announcements of bus departures blared over the public address system:

> May I have your attention please! The through bus to Dallas is now loading for Oakland, Modesto, Fresno, Bakersfield, Barstow, Albuquerque, Clovis, Sweetwater, and Dallas.

The steady rattle and hum of bus engines could be heard out back as passengers streamed through the glass doorways leading to the forty-six departure gates outside. Buses from Seattle, Chicago, New Orleans, New York, and other cities were rolling in and out of the depot one after another—the familiar Greyhound dog emblazoned on the side of each bus along with the emblematic sign that was urging everyone to "Discover America."

With all the weekend activity it had been easy to miss him. The balding, middle-aged man had been wandering aimlessly around the terminal before Charlie, our seventy-five-year-old retired engineer volunteer, brought him to my attention. When I approached the confused man, he was unable to tell me his name or where he was from. Remaining silent as I continued to gently question him, he eventually reached into his pocket and pulled out a ticket stub from Reno, Nevada, and a key of some sort.

When I asked if he lived in Reno, he nodded his head "Yes." Then, with halting speech, he began to respond to some of my questions. He said he came to San Francisco because he was "tired of watching TV." The key he was holding in his hand was for his "room" in Reno. When I asked if he wanted to return to Reno, he answered with another "Yes." San Francisco may have looked good when he was bored in Reno, but now he wanted to go back home. However, before I could help him I needed to learn his name and to confirm he was really from Reno and that he actually had a room there. This was no easy task, given that he appeared to be developmentally disabled and was without any money or personal identification. Yet somehow we needed to come up with a plan. It was our Travelers Aid policy not to send anyone anywhere without a definite plan.

We refused to do the "Greyhound therapy" that other towns and cities frequently employed. Greyhound therapy was when an agency or organization gave someone a free one-way bus ticket to a distant town or city *just* to get rid of them—with little or no concern about what happened to them once they arrived. The whole idea was to get a homeless or "problem" person out of their area as fast as possible. Some recipients were instructed to go right to Travelers Aid when they reached their destination. Because San Francisco was regarded as one of the country's more "tolerant" cities, we were a popular dumping ground for these Greyhound therapy recipients. I saw many of them when they arrived at the bus station.

To avoid this kind of poor case management, Travelers Aid always developed a realistic plan for the people we were trying to help. And that was why I needed to talk with someone— anyone—who could shed some light on this mystery man with the Nevada ticket stub. But the man I was now calling "Reno" still couldn't tell me his name, much less the name of anyone he might know in Nevada. After getting him something to eat, I would have to refer him to Adult Protective Services.

However, while eating at the Greyhound coffee shop, "Reno" happened to mention an "Ace Liquor Store." Seizing on this possible clue, I called Nevada information when we returned to the Travelers Aid booth and was given a number for the one and only Ace Liquor Store in Reno. I phoned the store, described "Reno" to the manager, and asked if he happened to know him. "Oh sure," he replied, "Everybody knows Paul. Is he okay?"

After I explained the situation, he recalled that Paul had taken a bus to San Francisco in a similar manner a year or two previous. He said Paul was "mildly retarded," but lived in his own apartment near the liquor store. An agency worker visited Paul weekly to assist him with his independent living skills. The store manager noted that people in the neighborhood liked Paul and were always doing little things to help him out.

When I mentioned that Paul didn't have any money, the manager said they would take up a collection at the store to bring him back home. I told him he could prepay Paul's ticket at the Reno Greyhound and they would wire the ticket on to San Francisco. I also let him know that Travelers Aid would authorize a 25% reduction in the fare and that we'd notify Reno Greyhound about the discount before he bought the ticket. He said he would purchase the ticket as soon as he raised the money and that he'd be there to meet Paul when his bus arrived in Reno.

Two hours later, a Greyhound ticket agent informed me that Paul's bus ticket had been wired. After getting the ticket, I called the store manager to confirm the arrival time. He said several neighbors would keep an eye on Paul until his social worker was contacted Monday morning. When I thanked him for everything they were doing, he said they were glad to help out.

Making sure Paul had food for the trip, I then walked him out to his bus. He seemed very relieved to be going home. After giving the driver a heads-up, I said good-bye to Paul and wished him well. Moments later he was headed home to Reno and his devoted friends.

Paul's crisis had been simply resolved—thanks to a good neighbor. Another developmentally disabled client's crisis would also be simply resolved—thanks to a good neighbor. The Oklahoma Kid was something else.

The Oklahoma Kid

As a bird that wandereth from her nest,
so is a man that wandereth from his place.

—Proverbs 27:8

Everyone's heart went out to the young man with cerebral palsy. He had limited use of his left arm, limped slightly, and his speech was muddled and hard to understand. Our volunteer Joel, a department store CEO doing community-service hours, had seen the young man at our Travelers Aid booth before referring him to me. It took some time before I learned his name was Frankie Taylor and that he was from Oklahoma. It was difficult finding out anything else about him.

Frankie was black and appeared to be in his mid-teens, but he might have been older. He had a disarming smile and humble way about him that was quite endearing. Like Paul from Reno, he had no money or identification. From the little I could pick up, Frankie had probably run away from home or some kind of institutional care in Oklahoma. And while I struggled to understand him, he seemed to have no trouble understanding me.

I decided to wait before calling the San Francisco Department of Social Services, sensing he might run if he thought I was calling the authorities. My inclination was to get him out of the Tenderloin and into a more protective setting where he wouldn't be in such immediate danger of being exploited. Perhaps a sympathetic care provider could gain Frankie's confidence, learn more about him, and help us understand what was going on. I told Frankie, if he was willing, Travelers Aid would house him at a local board and care home. When he surprisingly agreed, I had him sit in the lobby while I made some calls to local care providers.

It took a while, but eventually I found a care provider who was willing to take him. Her home was in the city's predominantly black Western Addition. She would house him on a day-to-day basis and we would reimburse her at the prevailing board and care rate. She would even drive down to the Greyhound to pick him up.

After making these arrangements, I found Frankie playing pinball across the lobby. He was entertaining some of the Greyhound regulars with his surprisingly adept pinball skills. Even with the limited use of his left arm, he was able to manipulate the flippers with amazing agility. He had clearly gained the respect of those gathered around him as he racked up points.

"Atta baby!" someone shouted. "Way to go!" another exclaimed. The "Oklahoma Kid" was quite a hit with the local Greyhound gang. He had apparently played his first game with a donated quarter and bells had been ringing and free games popping up ever since. Obviously alluding to The Who and their rock opera *Tommy*, someone referred to Frankie as a "pinball wizard." And while the crowd could barely understand him, there was a lot of heart-to-heart communication going on. Frankie had a way about him.

When he finished his last game, Frankie and I sat down in the lobby. I explained how I'd found a temporary home for him and that the care provider was on her way to the bus station to meet him. He would stay with her until we came up with a better plan. She arrived thirty minutes later and Frankie seemed to like her right away. As they left the bus station, I hoped she would gain his confidence and learn more about him.

Several days later the care operator called to let me know there'd been a startling turn of events regarding Frankie. With a smile in her voice, she described how she and Frankie were sitting on her front porch when Frankie's mother—yes, Frankie's mother—happened to drive by and see him sitting there. Joining them on the porch, his mother told the care provider that Frankie and the rest of her family lived several blocks away in that very same neighborhood! It turned out that Frankie was *born* in Oklahoma, but their family had moved to San Francisco five years before. She showed the astonished care provider a photograph of Frankie and the family, along with her California driver's license listing their nearby address.

His mother explained that while Frankie was developmentally disabled, he was very "street smart." Two or three times a year when he became especially bored, he would take off on what she called his "adventures." Showing up in different parts of the city, he told people he was from Oklahoma and received lots of attention—just as he had from Travelers Aid. She wasn't surprised to hear that he had won everyone's heart down at the Greyhound. She said she tried to keep an eye on him, but sometimes he would just slip away.

While his mother was concerned he might get hurt some day on one of his adventures, she and the care provider still had a good laugh about what happened. What were the odds that a Travelers Aid social worker would house the "Oklahoma Kid" right in the middle of his own San Francisco neighborhood!

With Frankie, it had literally been "California here I come, right back where I started from." Several months later, a Greyhound drunk would sing his own rendition of this very same song.

The Greyhound Crooner

Now unto him that is able to keep you from falling...

—Jude 24

Dressed in a coat and tie, the obviously intoxicated middle-aged man stepped up to the Travelers Aid booth and broke into loud song. He had the attention of the whole Greyhound lobby as he bellowed, "California here I come, right back where I started from!" before suddenly crashing to the floor. Lying flat on his back in front of our Travelers Aid booth, he was out cold.

In cases like these, I didn't call the police; I called the Mobile Assistance Patrol. This volunteer group, largely comprised of recovered alcoholics, would take the man to a supportive detoxification center rather than the city jail. My Bernal Heights neighbor, Ernie, a local attorney and a recovered alcoholic himself, was the MAP volunteer who came by this day to take our Greyhound crooner to detox. I was continually impressed with how Ernie and the other MAP volunteers performed their work so patiently—always according dignity to their clients, no matter how drunk or disheveled they might be.

After greeting me, Ernie gently roused the inebriated man and helped him to his feet. He slowly and carefully led him out to the MAP van that was parked in front of the Greyhound. From previous conversations I knew Ernie's thinking in situations like these: "There but by the grace of God go I." Uttered by some folks, that statement can seem quite condescending and patronizing. But when stated by people like Ernie, it conveyed nothing but respect for the people they were serving. He realized with a little twist or turn in his own life, it could easily have been *him* lying on that floor. That was why I always called the Mobile Assistance Patrol for people like our Greyhound crooner.

But who do you call for a "drunken" policeman? The police? In my case, I ended up calling the local newspaper.

The "Drunken" Policeman

And lead us not into temptation...
—Matthew 6:13

Walking up Leavenworth Street on my way to the Coronado Hotel, I saw a confused man in baggy clothes staggering in the middle of the sidewalk. Bobbing and weaving precariously, he appeared to be drunk or high on drugs. Concerned that he might walk into traffic or fall and hit his head, I approached him and asked, "Hey man, are you okay?"

He made no response as he continued swaying from side to side. When I came closer, he fell forward into my arms. I had to hold him to keep him from tumbling into the street. With both of my arms wrapped around him—he was very large—I tried to steer him over to the steps of a nearby apartment building and out of harm's way. But now, with all his weight upon me, he started bobbing and weaving again. I continued talking to him in hopes of eliciting *some* kind of response, but it was everything I could do to keep us both from collapsing to the ground. We had to be quite a sight as we swayed back and forth doing our Tenderloin two-step.

While holding on to him, I noticed my right hand was just inches away from a wad of bills that protruded from the wallet in his back pocket. After another few minutes of his rocking back and forth—and my continuing efforts to make sure he was all right—I finally got my answer.

Uttering a string of expletives under his breath, he told me in no uncertain terms to leave him alone. But his voice was surprisingly clear and sober. Shocked more by his sobriety than his profane outburst, I immediately dropped my arms and walked away as he resumed staggering and stumbling down the sidewalk. I was really confused.

A male transvestite with a red ribbon in his hair was sitting on a nearby stoop taking this all in. As I passed by, he smiled sympathetically and apologized for not saying anything. "That was a cop, honey. He *wanted* you to take his money. But if I told you who he was and what he was doing, he would have arrested me."

Suddenly I understood what was going on. The man I had been trying to help was a police "decoy." I knew that local police officers had recently gone undercover to protect vulnerable inner-city residents from being robbed. But *this* was how they were doing it?

Later as I returned to the bus station, I saw another man in baggy clothes lying on the sidewalk at Seventh and Market. A bulging wallet was sticking out of his back pocket. Normally I would call the Mobile Assistance Patrol when someone seemed to be down and out like this. But realizing he was just another undercover policeman, I called the *San Francisco Examiner* newspaper instead of MAP.

When I reached a reporter at the city desk, I described the two decoys I'd encountered, the frustration evident in my voice. There *had* to be a better way for San Francisco police to fight crime in the Tenderloin. While attempting to smoke out the bad guys, they were actually tempting the poorest of the city's poor with their easy money and unnecessarily involving people like myself who were trying to help—it made no sense at all. The reporter told me they'd received a number of complaints like mine. In fact, the *Examiner* was about to do an article on the dubious ethics of police entrapment. The issue wasn't about police attempting to protect Tenderloin residents; it was the *way* they were going about it. The paper eventually ran a hard-hitting article about the decoys.

Ultimately, public uproar brought this kind of police entrapment to a halt—but not before one of our Travelers Aid clients succumbed to this questionable scheme.

Tyrone

Watch and pray, that ye enter not into temptation:
the spirit indeed is willing, but the flesh is weak.

—Matthew 26:41

Tyrone came to the Greyhound one Saturday morning. A young African-American in his early twenties, he had a bright smile and a surprisingly upbeat attitude for someone who was homeless. He'd recently arrived from New York City, full of high expectations. But now, having exhausted his meager savings looking for work, he wasn't sure what to do next—maybe go back to New York. Someone on the street had referred him to Travelers Aid.

Part of my job was trouble-shooting with newly arrived clients like Tyrone. After a lengthy discussion he decided—with Travelers Aid support—to give the San Francisco job market one more chance. I gave him some ideas for work and told him we would house him at the Coronado Hotel for the next three days. This inexpensive, no-frills Tenderloin hotel was located just five blocks from the Greyhound on Ellis Street. It was owned by the Patels, a close-knit Indian family that lived on the second floor. Travelers Aid had an ongoing contract with the Coronado for several rooms, including a family room.

Owner Victor Patel was my main contact at the Coronado. During my two years with Travelers Aid, I saw Victor, his wife Sandha, and their two sons, Robert and Roger, on an almost daily basis. Victor and his family were part of a large local Hindu community that often gathered at their Indian social hall in the Tenderloin for weddings and special events. Home-cooked food was an important part of their celebrations and family life. Thanks to the Patels, I became very fond of Indian food.

If I was at the Coronado Hotel at dinnertime, Mr. Patel usually invited me to dine with him and his family. In his broken English he would say, "Warren—eat?" While Sandha made chapatis and served curries and other delectable Indian fare, Victor and I sat on the floor at a low table, enjoying our food while discussing our mutual Travelers Aid clients.

I phoned Mr. Patel to let him know Tyrone would be staying in one of our rooms for the next three nights. I told Tyrone if he checked back with me on Tuesday, I could probably extend his stay another three days. As he left the depot with the vouchers I'd given him, I had a good feeling about Tyrone. He seemed motivated and determined, and I figured it would be just a matter of time before he found a job. In the meantime he would apply for assistance at the Department of Social Services as a back-up plan.

I was surprised when Tyrone didn't return that next Tuesday. Three weeks later he finally showed up at the Greyhound, but this time he looked tired and depressed. Gone was the ready smile and boyish optimism that had been so present in our previous meeting. Glad to see him but wondering why he seemed so down, I asked where he'd been. He hesitated a moment and then told me that he'd spent the last three weeks in jail.

On his second day at the Coronado, he felt cooped up and claustrophobic and *had* to get out of his room. Because it was a Sunday there wasn't much he could do in the way of looking for work, so he walked around all afternoon and well into the night. He was extremely hungry and almost delirious when he encountered a drunk passed out on a sidewalk near skid row. Tyrone noticed that a wallet with a wad of bills was sticking out of the man's back pocket. In his desperate state of mind, he convinced himself that it would be all right to take the man's money because if he didn't, someone else would.

"So," I said matter-of-factly, "you rolled a San Francisco cop."

Tyrone looked surprised and asked how I knew. I related my recent experience with the "drunken" policeman—how I had even called the paper to report how the police were tempting everyone with their "easy money." Then, looking right at Tyrone, I said, "But…"

"But I shouldn't be taking anyone's money, no matter what," he quickly interjected. I nodded my head sympathetically, but in obvious agreement. It was clear Tyrone was still upset with himself. He said he couldn't remember the last time he'd taken anything from anyone—even as a kid—and that he'd come to the Greyhound to apologize and explain why he had disappeared. He wanted me to know he was grateful for our assistance and that he was not a thief at heart. He told me he'd learned a tough lesson about trying to rationalize one's actions in the midst of hard times.

But as he turned to walk away, I asked him to wait. If he was willing to give it another try, Travelers Aid would put him back at the Coronado for another three nights—along with food vouchers for the same period of time so he could resume his search for employment. At first he refused—he'd come to apologize, not to ask for more help. I told him I appreciated his feelings, but encouraged him to keep working with us.

Amazed at being given another chance, he accepted my offer—Travelers Aid would house him again at the Coronado. During that time he would continue looking for work and also contact the San Francisco Department of Social Services to apply for Emergency General Assistance (GA). The GA would take effect within three days, providing him with basic food and housing until he found a job.

The following Tuesday I was informed by Carol, one of our daytime social workers, that our contract room at Aquarius House was open. The Aquarius program was a great resource because it offered more than just temporary housing. It provided young adults with food, housing, and job support for up to thirty days and was located outside the Tenderloin in the inner Sunset area of the city. Our room was usually occupied, so this was a tremendous opportunity for Tyrone.

That night, I went to see Tyrone at the Coronado and told him about the opening at Aquarius House. He was *very* interested in going there. As our liaison to the program, Carol made all the necessary arrangements the next afternoon. The following day, Tyrone was off on a city bus to Aquarius.

Two weeks later, Tyrone called to tell me he had been accepted into a training program at a local bank. He sounded really optimistic. As I hung up the phone, I wished we had more resources like Aquarius House. Travelers Aid was set up for short-term crisis intervention, not the month-long housing and career development offered by places like Aquarius. That was why networking and community referrals were so important. We all had a role to play in helping people in need.

I didn't hear anything more from Tyrone after that phone call. However, several months later, as I walked by the Bank of America near city hall, I heard someone shouting my name. When I turned around, I saw Tyrone bounding out of the bank in a business suit. Smiling broadly and pumping my hand enthusiastically, he gave me the big news. "Things are good, man! I'm working for Bank of America and my job is great! I even have my own apartment!" He was definitely a happy man.

We were both a bit overwhelmed by our unexpected meeting. He thanked me and Travelers Aid for hanging in there with him—he loved living and working in San Francisco and his life finally felt like it was going in the right direction. After talking another minute or so, he flashed that winning smile and said he had to get back to work. I gave him a hug and told him I was real proud of him.

As I walked back toward Market Street and the bus station, I thought of how rarely we saw clients after working with them. But every so often when we bumped into someone like Tyrone, it reminded us that hope really does spring eternal down at the Greyhound.

While Tyrone became fully employed in his second *month* in the city, fellow New Yorker Steven Jennings became fully employed on his second *day* in the city.

The Bricklayer

The labourer is worthy of his reward.
—1 Timothy 5:18

Steven Jennings, his wife, and their two children had hitchhiked out to San Francisco from upper New York State. He was a bricklayer but work had been slow. In the past he'd supplemented his family's income by trapping game in the wintertime, but this year the creeks were frozen solid and all the animals had disappeared. They had no choice but to move to an area where he could find work as a bricklayer all year long. At Travelers Aid we encountered many families who were forced to move due to loss of their livelihood.

The family arrived in San Francisco with their last five dollars and a single suitcase of basic belongings. Someone on the street told them to contact Travelers Aid. Steven was calling from a pay phone on Mason Street to ask for help. I quickly left the Greyhound and met the family at the phone booth.

Steven described how a Bay Area bricklayer had picked them up on the highway and had given them a ride to Reno several days before. The bricklayer had business in Reno, but told Steven to call him when they arrived in San Francisco—maybe he could help. Steven had just phoned him, but apparently the man wasn't home yet. He would try to reach him again the next day. In the meantime, I assured Steven that Travelers Aid would provide them with emergency food and housing for the night. Handing him the necessary vouchers for food and a family room at the YMCA Hotel, I asked him to meet me the next day at the Greyhound so we could work on a short-term plan.

The following morning Steven called. He had just spoken with the Bay Area bricklayer and their new friend was on his way to pick them up at the YMCA Hotel. The local bricklayer had already lined up a job for Steven and found a place for Steven's family to stay with one of his friends. They had eaten breakfast and were about to leave the hotel. Everything seemed to be working out. Steven thanked us for our help and we said good-bye. As I hung up the phone I wished it could always be that easy.

While the Jennings' unexpected help enabled them to stay in the San Francisco Bay Area, the Thompson family's unexpected help made it possible for them to return to Tennessee.

The Tennessee Thompsons

In everything give thanks...
—1 Thessalonians 5:18

The family was straight out of a John Steinbeck novel. Their story was a southern-fried *Grapes of Wrath* saga with an upside-down, only-in-San Francisco, Horatio Alger twist. It was the tale of a dirt-poor Tennessee family named Thompson that traveled out to California on a Greyhound bus to seek their fortune. Standing in front of the Travelers Aid booth, Mr. Thompson confidently affirmed his family's intentions: "Sir, we heard that a man could make a heap of change out here in California and we aim to get a piece of that change."

The slow-talking, slow-moving, Mr. Thompson was in his early thirties. His whole demeanor was reminiscent of those hot, humid summer afternoons in the South when everything seems to move in slow motion. He described how he, his wife, and their three young children came out West from Tennessee. His goal was to make enough money to return to Tennessee to buy some land, hook up a trailer, and eventually build a home. But Mr. Thompson explained there were a few immediate obstacles—namely, they'd used up all of their savings getting to California and now they had no money, no food, and no place to stay. They were in serious trouble.

After talking with Mr. Thompson, I was sure the family would be eligible for emergency assistance from the Department of Social Services. Because none of the family shelters had room, I gave them vouchers for a three-night stay at the Coronado Hotel and for some food at Lunardi's Grocery. I also provided

Mr. Thompson with a list of local employment agencies, along with some community resources they would find helpful.

I called Mr. Patel to let him know the Thompsons would be staying in our family room. Since they had several large suitcases, I put the family in a cab to the Coronado and paid their fare. I asked Mr. Thompson to check back in several days to let me know how things were going.

Watching the cab pull away, I was reminded of the depression families that Woody Guthrie sang about. The Thompsons were like a modern-day, dust-bowl family with a big dust-bowl type dream—and almost nothing else. They were going to need a lot of help—and a lot of luck—if they were to ever make it back to Tennessee with that much-hoped-for "piece-of-change."

Three days later, Mr. Thompson came by the Greyhound to inform me the family was now receiving aid from the Department of Social Services. With their food and housing covered, they no longer needed our assistance in those areas. He thanked me for being so "neighborly" and said he would stay in touch as he looked for work.

The following week Mr. Thompson returned to the Greyhound again. I was surprised to see him limping. He grimaced as he greeted me and was in obvious pain. He told me that the previous day he had been grazed by a city bus as he was crossing Market Street. The driver had braked hard but Mr. Thompson was hit by the bus. He was feeling some pain in his back and leg. Witnesses had informed police that the bus driver was at fault.

The city's insurance people were immediately on the scene and had offered him $300 to sign a release. But he told them he wouldn't do anything until he'd talked to his Travelers Aid social worker. He'd come to the Greyhound to ask me what he should do.

I told him not to sign anything until he had a complete physical and talked with a lawyer. If there was anything seriously wrong with him, the money offered by the city surely wouldn't be adequate, especially if the injury affected his ability to work. I advised him to get over to San Francisco General Hospital so he could be examined.

Mr. Thompson returned the next day to report on his trip to the hospital. The attending physician informed him that he had suffered some definite damage to his back. Realizing it was time for an attorney, I referred the weary Mr. Thompson to Neighborhood Legal Services. They would be the best ones to help him deal with the city's insurance people.

The next week, Mr. Thompson came to see me one last time. He said that Neighborhood Legal Services had been very helpful. He had received a generous settlement from the insurance company. The family now had enough money to return to Tennessee to buy their land and hook up a trailer. In fact, they were taking a Greyhound bus home the next day.

Listening to his account, I tried to comprehend the full scope of what had just happened. In less than three weeks, the Thompsons' California dream had actually come true. They got their "piece of change" and were heading back to Tennessee to buy their land. Tenderloin con artists couldn't have devised a more perfect scheme. But the Thompsons hadn't conned anyone. Circumstances had just uniquely conspired to give them exactly what they'd hoped for.

In his song, "Do-Re-Mi," Woody Guthrie warned of the danger of trying to get to California without any money during the dust-bowl years. He sang:

> *Oh, if you ain't got the do re mi, boys,*
> *you ain't got the do re mi,*
> *Why, you better go back to beautiful Texas,*
> *Oklahoma, Kansas, Georgia, Tennessee.*

In the Thompson's unique twist on this Guthrie song, they went to California *without* the "do re mi" but were now returning to Tennessee *with* the "do re mi." After Mr. Thompson shook my hand and thanked Travelers Aid and me one final time, we said good-bye. As he walked out of the bus station I had to smile. I was picturing Mr. Thompson in the future, in a rocking chair on his front porch, looking over his land and telling his grandchildren how he'd traveled to California to seek his fortune. That he heard there was a "heap of change" out there and how he'd gotten "a piece of that change." What Mr. Thompson will never know, however, is that if I'd referred him to San Francisco's famed personal injury lawyer, Melvin Belli, instead of Neighborhood Legal Services, he might have been able to buy Graceland or maybe even the Grand Ole Opry.

While a San Francisco municipal bus was instrumental in helping the Thompsons get back to Tennessee, those same San Francisco buses prevented Lily Price from going anywhere.

Lily

I was in prison, and ye came unto me.

—Matthew 25:36

Public transportation was at a standstill on San Francisco city streets. A massive strike by municipal bus drivers had paralyzed the whole Bay Area as union carriers were respecting the local picket lines. To get almost anywhere you had to drive a car, take a cab, ride a bike, or walk. Not what you expect when you fly in from out of town—especially if you're trying to get from the Greyhound bus station out to neighboring Marin County.

Lily Price was visibly shaken and confused. The frail, seventy-two-year-old grandmother came to our Travelers Aid booth when she arrived at the bus station and learned of the strike. She'd flown in from San Diego to surprise her nephew on his birthday; he was an inmate at San Quentin State Prison some eighteen miles away. She'd been able to take a Greyhound bus in from the airport as Greyhound drivers weren't striking with the local city bus drivers—but Greyhound didn't serve Marin County.

With the strike on and a small Social Security check as her only income, those eighteen miles suddenly seemed like a thousand. Her travel budget had been based on riding the inexpensive Marin County Transit bus from San Francisco to Marin County and then taking the short cab ride to the prison. However, because of the strike the Marin County buses weren't running, and round-trip cab fare from the city to San Quentin was out of the question. Her plane ticket alone had taken most of her meager Social Security check. Overwhelmed and nearly in tears, she said she would just fly back home the next afternoon as planned—but without having seen her nephew. She would have to visit him another time.

With her travel plans unraveling at the seams, she asked me to please cancel her motel reservation near the prison and to help her find an inexpensive place to stay near the bus station. I told her I would, but first I wanted to see if there wasn't *some* way to get her to San Quentin. There were a number of prisoner support groups in the city—maybe one of them provided rides for families.

I asked Lily to sit in the lobby while I called around. For the next twenty minutes I spoke with every known prisoner support group in the San Francisco Bay Area—Friends Outside, Prisoner's Forum, the Northern California Service League, and even San Quentin itself—all to no avail. None of them had volunteer drivers or offered any kind of transportation to the prison.

At one point I looked over at Lily. She looked so alone and distraught sitting there in the Greyhound lobby. Flying to San Francisco had been taxing, but the disappointment of not seeing her nephew was almost too much for her. It was right at that moment I remembered my plans for the next day and suddenly realized I had the perfect solution. As a part of that solution, I phoned the manager of the Arlington Hotel. After talking with him, I called out to Lily.

"Lily, come here! I've found you a ride and a place to stay!"

Rising slowly from her seat, she walked over to hear the details. I explained that she had a ride, but it didn't leave until the next morning. I also told her I'd made a reservation for her at the nearby Arlington Hotel. Because the manager had been sympathetic to her plight she would be paying next to nothing for her room. She was delighted yet puzzled. "But who is giving me a ride to San Quentin?" she wanted to know.

"Well," I said a bit awkwardly, "I'm your ride."

At first Lily would have nothing to do with it. She said she wouldn't let me go out of my way like that. But she began to soften when I told her I really wasn't going out of my way—

that I'd already planned to go hiking the next day on Mount Tamalpais with a friend. Pulling out a map of the area, I showed her how close Mount Tamalpais was to San Quentin.

It was simple. I would pick her up at her hotel in the morning and take her to San Quentin before meeting my friend. After my hike, I would return to the prison and drive her to the airport to make her scheduled flight. The San Francisco Airport was only fifteen minutes from my apartment. Seeing it neatly laid out like that, she gave in and accepted my offer. With our plan now in motion, I put Lily in a cab for the short ride over to the Arlington Hotel. I suggested she eat an early dinner; the area could be especially dangerous after dark.

The next morning, I drove through a sleepy Tenderloin that was enveloped in fog. The streets were quiet and empty. The only people around were probably heading to the morning mass at St. Boniface Church. When I arrived at the hotel, Lily was waiting in the lobby with her one large suitcase. It probably contained more gifts for her nephew than it did her own belongings. This unassuming lady was truly from another era. After helping her into my VW "Beetle", I drove up Ellis Street, took a right on Van Ness Avenue, then a left down Lombard. Minutes later we were heading out across the Golden Gate Bridge. The sun was starting to break through the fog and weekend sailboats were already weaving their way around the Bay. It promised to be a great day.

Over in Marin County we drove past Sausalito and Mill Valley before exiting Highway 101 past the town of Corte Madera. Rolling hills framed the countryside across from the prison. Standing high on a particular rise in Corte Madera, one could see San Francisco's skyline to the south and San Quentin Prison to the north. From a distance the prison was more picturesque than intimidating.

Moments later we reached the gates of San Quentin. Behind its foreboding walls, an unsuspecting prisoner was about to have a surprise birthday visit from his devoted aunt. After accompanying Lily to the visitors' center and making sure she was cleared, I told her I'd be back to pick her up in three hours.

Returning to the prison after my hike, I found Lily waiting in the reception area. Smiling and obviously happy, she described the "wonderful" visit she had with her nephew. He'd been surprised to see her, was grateful for all the gifts, and had some encouraging news—if all went well he would be released in less than a year.

While driving back on Highway 101 toward the Golden Gate Bridge, Lily told me I was now her "adopted grandson." With her voice breaking, she said the last two years since her husband died had been especially hard. She had lost her faith in people, but the events of the last day had helped to change that. She said she was deeply appreciative to Travelers Aid and for my willingness to help her on my day off.

When we arrived at the airport, Lily kissed me on the cheek and promised I would be hearing from her. Six weeks later I received a package in the mail. Inside the neatly wrapped parcel was a beautiful multi-colored quilt that had been hand-stitched by my "adopted grandmother."

Most people driving by San Quentin Prison probably think of all the hardened criminals locked up inside. Whenever I drive by San Quentin, I think of the loving kindness that Lily brought, not only to a grateful nephew, but also to a grateful social worker.

While seventy-two-year-old Lily Price's plans all worked out in the end, seventy-three-year-old Willis Potter's plan was to end it all.

Willis Potter

My kinsfolk have failed, and my familiar
friends have forgotten me.

—Job 19:14

When I first spoke with Willis Potter, he had been sitting in the Greyhound lobby for nearly three days. He'd caught the attention of our volunteer as he periodically walked past the Travelers Aid booth to go up the stairs to the men's room on the second floor. A North Carolina native, the seventy-three-year-old man wore wire-rimmed glasses, spoke with a strong southern accent, and walked with a noticeable stoop. His thin, silvery-gray hair framed his high pale forehead and angular facial features. Wearing a coat and tie and neatly shined shoes, Mr. Potter was very proper in his own country kind of way. His manner was gruff and he would periodically punctuate his sentences with the characteristic phrase, "Don't ya know."

"I spent my whole life in Holly Hill, don't ya know. I was livin' with my sister there until she died two years ago. Her kinfolk kicked me out after she died. They tried to put me in a home for old fogeys, don't ya know. But I ran away to New York. I met a Jewish woman there and lived in her home near Coney Island. Then one day we had a fight and I had to leave, don't ya know. Been travelin' ever since." He told me how he'd crisscrossed the country several times over the past two years with his suitcase and three large trunks—but in spite of all his traveling he'd never found a place that felt like home.

"I miss them dogwoods in the spring, don't ya know. That Carolina countryside is the prettiest dang thing you'd ever want to see." His eyes seemed to glisten as he pictured the familiar scene in his mind. "But if I went back to Holly Hill they'd just try to stick me back in that home for old fogeys, don't ya know."

When I asked Mr. Potter what his plans were, he said, "To die." I was taken aback by his straightforward pronouncement and asked him to explain.

"I aim to die, blast it! I arrived here at this bus station with $65 and some hoodlum robbed me twenty minutes later, don't ya know. Social Security doesn't even know I'm here, and they never get my checks straight anyway. I'm sick of the whole thing. I had a good life, but it was over the day I left Holly Hill. I'm too old and too tired to keep travelin' around like this. I want to die, and this bus station is as good a place as any."

"Die right here in the Greyhound?" I asked incredulously.

"Yes, sir. Right here in the Greyhound. Living is too much dang trouble, don't ya know. I don't care anymore." He had made up his mind and that was that. The fact that he wasn't asking me or anyone else for assistance seemed to underscore the seriousness of his plan. For Mr. Potter, the San Francisco Greyhound bus station was the literal end of the line. While most people in the lobby were waiting for a bus, Mr. Potter was waiting to die.

"Mr. Potter, when was the last time you had something to eat?" I asked.

"Three days ago," he replied.

"Mr. Potter, you can't just sit here and die!"

"Watch me," he said with utter conviction.

I didn't want to call Adult Protective Services, but he wasn't leaving me much choice. Before taking that step, however, I made one last appeal by sharing a personal note about the city he now found himself in. I described my traveling out to San Francisco from Connecticut after being discharged from the Army. I was discouraged and depressed, but the city had given me hope and a new start. The people were friendly and open, and before long the city felt like home. I told him the reason I had my job in the bus station was because the people of San Francisco—through agencies such as United Way—wanted Travelers Aid to help people like him. I acknowledged that San

Francisco was not Holly Hill, but the city had its own special beauty and charm.

Continuing my plea, I urged Mr. Potter to give Travelers Aid a chance. We could provide him with food and lodging, help straighten out his Social Security, and refer him to the Tenderloin Senior Center for assistance with permanent housing. Instead of putting him in a "home for old fogeys," they would help him find his own apartment. I could even arrange to have Greyhound keep his trunks until he was settled.

Mr. Potter listened intently to everything I said. Perhaps too tired to offer any further resistance, he reluctantly agreed to work with me. I immediately took him over to the Greyhound coffee shop where he ended his three-day fast with a hamburger and a cherry Coke. After telling Greyhound to hold on to his three trunks, I called Mr. Patel and reserved a room for Mr. Potter at the Coronado. I then accompanied the weary North Carolina native in a cab to the hotel. After walking him to his room, I handed him several food vouchers. I told him to get some rest and that I'd be back the next day.

The following afternoon I led Mr. Potter over to the Senior Center on Leavenworth Street. Travelers Aid would work jointly with the center in assisting him. While they helped him find an apartment, we would continue to meet his immediate needs for food and lodging. We would also make sure that his Social Security payments were properly reinstated.

The Senior Center found him a small furnished apartment two blocks from the bus station in a building designed for seniors who were still able to live independently. The manager was very supportive and allowed Mr. Potter to move in right away, deferring the rent and deposit until his Social Security checks caught up with him. He even advanced Mr. Potter some money for his beloved "chewin' tobacco."

I was happy for Mr. Potter and visited him regularly during my dinner breaks. He would tell me tales about his childhood farm and of southern days gone by. Over time, I discovered he had his own unique vocabulary—he talked of his love for "cowpop" (milk) and his penchant for eating "cackleberries" (eggs). He was feisty and rarely smiled, but sometimes I detected a twinkle in his eyes when he delivered one of his characteristic digs at life today compared to "the good ole days." Mr. Potter liked to tease me by calling San Francisco "Frisco." I would remind him that San Franciscans *never* called San Francisco "Frisco." Referring to the city as "Frisco" was the sure sign of an outsider—and that he was no longer an outsider.

Mr. Potter lived in his apartment for about six months. The last time I saw him he said he was moving out of the Tenderloin. The Senior Center had found him a studio apartment near the ocean in the Richmond District, which he described as "real peaceful." The Tenderloin was too dangerous, he said, and now he wouldn't have to be so worried about getting robbed by "hoodlums." When I left his apartment that day, I was thankful that the man from Holly Hill would be living out the rest of his days in an apartment by the Pacific Ocean rather than in the lobby of the Greyhound bus station. His life had been uniquely shaped in the South, but Mr. Potter—"don't ya know"—was now a full-fledged San Franciscan.

And while some southerners like Mr. Potter permanently re-located in San Francisco, other southerners like Renee made San Francisco just a seasonal visit.

Renee

Ask, and it shall be given you…
—Matthew 7:7

Renee was fifty years old. Her black-rimmed glasses were a stark contrast to her pale white skin. With slightly graying dark hair and some well-worn wrinkles, she had a deep craggy voice and smelled heavily of cigarettes. She called New Orleans home. Making her living sketching caricatures in the French Quarter most of the year, she came to San Francisco to avoid the Louisiana winters.

Renee had recently arrived in the city and was staying in a nearby Tenderloin hotel. With surprising candor, she told me she'd gotten drunk the night before and spent the money she had set aside for art supplies. She knew it was asking a lot, but she was requesting we loan her five dollars to buy the chalk she needed to do the caricature work that paid her bills. The portfolio she showed me included humorous portraits of famous people like Marilyn Monroe and Elvis Presley. Preferring not to involve Travelers Aid, I told her I would personally pay for her chalk if she agreed to come back and do *my* caricature. When she readily agreed, I gave her the money and she headed off to the art store.

Thirty minutes later she returned with her newly purchased chalk and completed my sketch. At the bottom of her clever drawing, which she'd titled "The Travelers Aid Man," she included a little Greyhound bus. She thanked me for helping her out and I thanked her for giving me something to hang in the empty space above my desk. Moments later, with chalk and portfolio in hand, she said good-bye and left.

Several months later, when spring arrived, I knew she was probably back in New Orleans. It was easy to picture her sitting at her easel in Jackson Square, drinking a Dixie Beer and sketching tourists from around the world.

One night, in the fall of that same year, my pager sounded and I ducked into the Ritz Bar to use their pay phone. As the answering service patched me through to the caller, I looked above the bar and had to smile. Lining the wall were a number of familiarly drawn caricatures and Renee's signature was at the bottom of each picture. Tony Bennett may have left his heart in San Francisco, but Renee had left her wonderful drawings—and I imagined the customers of the Ritz Bar were as pleased with their caricatures as I was with mine.

But as one New Orleans client disappeared from the Tenderloin, another one arrived. Gino was someone I had known and worked with when I lived in New Orleans.

Gino

*The Lord watch between me and thee, when
we are absent one from another.*

—Genesis 31:49

Sometimes the world *really* is a small place. One afternoon, while working in our main office before heading down to the Greyhound, I did a double take when I saw Gino sitting in our waiting room. He looked up and was as surprised to see me as I was to see him. It had been over a year since we'd last seen each other in New Orleans where I was working my way through graduate school at Tulane University as the live-in counselor at a psychiatric halfway house. Gino was one of our fourteen residents—all of whom had serious mental problems. Most of them came straight from the state hospital across Lake Pontchartrain in Mandeville.

I took Gino back to my corner office where we reminisced about McKinney House and those of us who lived there—Bob and Joni the "house parents," Edna the quirky cook, me the resident social worker, and all the guys. We recalled super-macho Henry and the wry, cynical Tobias, each committing suicide within a year of leaving the halfway house. There was dark-skinned, "Pretty Boy" Sammy, with his mirrored platform shoes and his love of the French Quarter boys. And of course, there was Humberto "Baby Huey" Cabrero. I reminded Gino how, in one of our group meetings, each resident had to anonymously describe another group member as a car—and someone described the heavy, lethargic "Baby Huey" as "a '57 Chevy with four flat tires."

We laughed about super-serious, droopy-eyed Doug who invented a mysterious "mosquito gun" that was supposed to— but never did—rid the house of pesky mosquitoes. There was Big Bill, who would stand in the K&B drugstore obsessing on all the pros and cons of what particular brand of soap to buy. And who could forget Josh—our longhaired, guitar-strumming, wannabe hippie whose main regret in life was being too young to go to the Woodstock music festival or to Haight-Ashbury for the Summer of Love. Now here was Gino, from that same New Orleans halfway house, sitting right in front of me.

He had been a friendly but somewhat reclusive resident of McKinney House. My main memory of Gino was how he fixed up an old American Flyer bicycle someone donated to the halfway house. He loved that bike and rode it all over New Orleans. He was particularly fond of riding from our uptown location on Cherokee Street, through Audubon Park, out across Magazine and Tchoupitoulas Streets, and on up to the levee overlooking the Mississippi River. There he would sit for hours and watch the ships wind their way along the historic waterway.

Gino always had a certain restlessness about him, and it was this unsettled quality that brought him to San Francisco. He said he felt like he had to get out of New Orleans and travel for a while. He'd come to Travelers Aid because his recently forwarded disability check hadn't reached him yet. It was supposed to be at the post office the next day, but until then he was out of money— could we possibly help with food and lodging for one night?

He was extremely grateful when I gave him vouchers for food and a single night at the Coronado Hotel. Because he was ready to leave as soon as he had the vouchers in hand, I realized that the sentimentality about New Orleans and McKinney House had been mainly mine. After giving him directions to the hotel, we said good-bye and he was out the door.

As I sat in my office reflecting on Gino's surprise appearance, I marveled at how often I had been crossing paths in San Francisco with people from my past. When I arrived in the city I was amazed to find Hayden, one of my college roommates in

Philadelphia, stationed at the local Army base. He was living with his wife Arlene in the Sunset District only a mile or so from my apartment. Another Philadelphia friend, Gloria, was also living in the Sunset area and working as a nurse at UC Hospital. I spent many happy hours visiting with these friends.

Barbara, my classmate at Staples High School in Westport, Connecticut, was working as the editor of a local magazine and living in a nearby neighborhood. I bumped into another childhood friend, Dann, on the J streetcar one night after leaving the Greyhound; we'd played Little League baseball together in Westport and shared a crush on the same pig-tailed seventh-grade girl. Dann was managing a movie theater on Van Ness Avenue. Rick, also a Westport Little Leaguer, was coming out of the liquor store by the Greyhound late one evening. He was now a Bay Area lawyer.

I also encountered two more high school classmates from Westport—Bettina and Nancy. Incredibly, Nancy's former husband was the former boyfriend of my present girlfriend Anne. And while I was working the streets of San Francisco for Travelers Aid, another Westport boy, actor Michael Douglas, was also working the streets of San Francisco—but on the popular television series *Streets of San Francisco*.

Gino's appearance in San Francisco had proven once again the truth of the old adage—"It's a small world." And while another old adage stated that all roads led to Rome, back in those days it seemed that all roads led to San Francisco.

That it *is* a small world was further demonstrated to me in a dramatic way at the bus station one night when two old friends were suddenly—and unexpectedly—reunited in the Greyhound lobby.

Hetch Hetchy Friends

A friend loveth at all times, and a brother is born for adversity.

—Proverbs 17:17

The San Francisco-based Sierra Club's first president was the highly revered naturalist, author, and mighty mountaineer John Muir. He was instrumental in helping to establish Yosemite National Park. But his similar attempts to save the Hetch Hetchy Valley near Yosemite failed, and Congress authorized the construction of the O'Shaughnessy Dam in 1913.

Completed in 1923, the dam turned the beautiful Hetch Hetchy Valley into a reservoir that instantly destroyed the valley's natural cathedral-like beauty. The Hetch Hetchy Reservoir became—and still is—the primary water source for the city of San Francisco. John Muir never got over it—he died just one year after the dam was approved. Muir's beloved Hetch Hetchy Valley would be dammed, and as far as he was concerned the people responsible for the damming were "damned" for doing it. Later work on the dam became one of the many projects of President Franklin Delano Roosevelt's Depression-era Works Projects Administration (WPA). Hundreds of WPA workers were enlisted by the U.S. Government during the Depression to do additional structural work on the dam.

One night while I was talking to an old-timer named Hank at our Greyhound booth, he suddenly called out to another man who was passing through the lobby. When Hank rushed over, the man recognized him immediately and they greeted each other like the long-lost friends they actually were. Several minutes later, Hank returned to our booth and told me their story.

"Forty years ago, during some pretty hard times, John and I worked together on the Hetch Hetchy Dam for the WPA. We hadn't seen each other since—until tonight." He said they were both living in the Bay Area and had exchanged phone numbers so they could meet for lunch sometime in the near future.

There are times when family and friends plan to meet each other at airports, railroad stations, and bus stations. There are also these kinds of serendipitous encounters that just seem to come out of the blue. I appreciated being a part of Hank and John's Greyhound reunion and imagined that even Hetch Hetchy Dam foe John Muir would not begrudge them their spontaneous meeting. However, I had to believe that the *poetic* Muir would describe it as *poetic justice* if either of these Hetch Hetchy workers happened to choke a bit on the drinking water that would be set before them at their future lunch together—drinking water that originated from that "damned" dam he had fought so hard to prevent so many years ago.

Herb Caen, the beloved *San Francisco Chronicle* columnist, often included anecdotal stories like this Hetch Hetchy reunion in his daily newspaper column. Readers called in many of the items Caen wrote about, and though I didn't phone him about these two Hetch Hetchy friends, I did call him about something else.

Hyde Street cable car with Alcatraz in the distance
(Photo by John O'Neill)

Herb Caen and the French Tourists

A word fitly spoken is like apples of gold in pictures of silver.

—Proverbs 25:11

I'm not sure how it happened, but the Director of Travelers Aid was asked at the last minute to provide a tour guide for a busload of visiting French college students. Although we were a social service agency and not Gray Line Tours, most of us working at Travelers Aid knew the city of San Francisco well. I was asked to meet the tour bus across the Bay in Oakland early the next day. I was told my lack of French would not be a problem because most of the students spoke fairly good English.

The following morning, while it was still dark, I left my Bernal Heights apartment and drove into the Tenderloin. After parking in my usual lot, I walked to the BART (Bay Area Rapid Transit) Station in Hallidie Plaza to catch the underground train to Oakland. The below-street-level plaza was adjacent to the famous cable car turn-around at Powell and Market.

Hallidie Plaza was named after Andrew Hallidie, the man who established the San Francisco cable car system in 1873. Prior to 1900 there were over 500 cable cars covering a 110-mile network. To the delight of tourists and locals alike, more than forty cable cars still cover over ten miles of San Francisco roadway. Hallidie's cable cars were designated a National Historic Landmark by the U.S. Government in 1964, and San Francisco wouldn't be San Francisco without them. With such close proximity to the cable car turn-around, it was only natural that the plaza should be named after Andrew Hallidie.

The plaza served as an entryway to the BART Station and was a popular spot for folks to hang out. It was also the place where Red, the controversial Market Street evangelist, preached almost daily. Standing at the upper rail of the plaza on Market Street, he would shout down warnings to his captive audience sitting in the park below. In the midst of clanging cable car bells and barking newspaper vendors, people heard all about hell whether they liked it or not. Street musicians, mimes, jugglers, and other performers frequently competed with Red for people's attention in the plaza area.

Hallidie Plaza was also a frequent site for noontime concerts, special brown-bag lunch events, and other civic outings. In addition, the plaza housed the San Francisco Visitors Center, where tourists obtained maps, bus schedules, and other information about the city.

As I descended the stairway to the BART Station just before daybreak, I was surprised to see litter strewn all over the plaza area. Apparently there had been a brown-bag lunch event the previous day and no one had cleaned up afterwards. There were brown bags everywhere. When I reached the ground level and walked past the Visitors Center toward the BART Station, I noticed some of the bags seemed to be moving. I thought my eyes were deceiving me, but then I saw the long tails and furry rear ends protruding from the brown bags. The bags were moving because there were rats inside of them: Yesterday's brown-bag lunch had become today's brown-bag breakfast for the downtown rat population. The rats couldn't have cared less about Rice-A-Roni—they had their own "San Francisco treat."

I watched the rats darting in and out of the lunch bags as they scampered around the plaza and over by the Visitors Center. Several were having a hard time and seemed to be stuck in their bags. Spinning in small circles, they were awkwardly trying to back away from their early morning meal. The whole scene might have been comical if it wasn't so bizarre. I felt like I was in the middle of *Willard*, the horror movie about rats. The plaza rats seemed to be everywhere and they were having a field day.

As I weaved my way through this surreal breakfast party, I tried to picture the unsuspecting tourists who would be arriving at the Visitors Center area in several hours—it was hardly the image the Chamber of Commerce had in mind for the elderly couple vacationing from Peoria. Only when I entered the BART Station and was away from this eerie scene was I able to breathe a sigh of relief.

After taking the eleven-minute subway ride under the San Francisco Bay to Oakland, I arrived at Jack London Square and grabbed a bite to eat before walking over to meet the tour bus. The group had requested I start the tour from the Oakland side of the Bay. From what I had just seen in Hallidie Plaza, I was glad they weren't beginning their tour at the San Francisco Visitors Center.

I was introduced to the students as "Monsieur Smith" from Travelers Aid. Leaving Oakland and crossing the Bay Bridge, we made our way around the city. I quickly learned the group was far more interested in where the rock group Jefferson Airplane played in Golden Gate Park than they were in the park itself. So while we made it to traditional tourist spots like Twin Peaks, Fisherman's Wharf, Coit Tower, Chinatown, the Hyde Street cable car line, and the Golden Gate Bridge, I also incorporated more San Francisco Americana into the tour to meet their obvious interest in the city's pop culture.

As we drove through North Beach, I pointed out poet Lawrence Ferlinghetti's City Lights Bookstore. I described the "beat" movement that emerged in North Beach around his bookstore and how *San Francisco Chronicle* columnist Herb Caen had coined the term "beatnik." When we went by Ghirardelli Square and Fisherman's Wharf, I told them about Grimes Poznikov—San Francisco's own "Automatic Human Jukebox." This delightful and creative offbeat musician was loved by nearly everyone. Poznikov amused his appreciative audience members— young and old alike—by suddenly appearing in the window-like stage area of his painted, refrigerator carton "juke box" with a kazoo or trumpet in hand. Colorfully dressed and sporting a fedora, the bearded, long-haired musician would pop up from inside his self-contained juke box to play requested tunes—but *only* after money was deposited in the designated slot on the side of his box. The performance you'd see depended on how much money was inserted. Reporter Kevin Fagan recalled Poznikov's routine in a November 1, 2005 *San Francisco Chronicle* article:

> The quality of the song depended on how much cash was dropped in the slot. A reporter selected "I Left My Heart in San Francisco" one hot summer day in 1976, slid in a dime, and got one quick kazoo blast. The reporter then tossed in $2, and when the performance lid flipped open Mr. Poznikov blew a soulful, pitch-perfect version of the same song on trumpet, fetching cheers from the crowd of 40 people gathered around.

On a more somber note, I pointed out the Federal Building where kidnapped heiress Patty Hearst's bank robbery trial had recently taken place. And as we drove by City Hall, I told them about "Jesus Christ Satan"—a local character who wore lipstick and paraded around town barefoot in a flowing robe, waving a large United Nations banner while cradling his little dog. The students were shocked to hear that he'd run for the city's Board of Supervisors several years before. Herb Caen mentioned in one of his columns that Jesus Christ Satan had been barred from attending even the liberal Unitarian Church on Franklin Street. He wrote:

> First Unitarian on Franklin, renowned for its generous attitude, has barred Jesus Christ Satan after the latter showed up at a service swinging a can of gasoline and cracking a whip.

I told the students that while Jesus Christ Satan lost his bid for office, San Francisco's infamous "Emperor Norton" circumvented the electoral process altogether. In 1859, the eccentric and insane Joshua Norton, rather than running for political office, simply declared himself the "Emperor of these United States" and the

"Protector of Mexico." A formerly successful businessman, Norton was a San Francisco Gold Rush figure who, despite losing both his fortune and his mind, went on to become one of San Francisco's most popular and endearing historical figures. Most of the local citizenry humored him by going along with his regal routine, calling him "Emperor." Many restaurants and local businesses honored the creative but worthless script that Norton issued in his own name. When he died in 1880, the city turned out en masse to mourn their beloved "Emperor."

While the French students did enjoy some of the more traditional aspects of the city, the definite highlight of the tour for them was visiting the Haight-Ashbury district. After my describing the 1967 Summer of Love and the many rock bands that played in those days, there was a reverential hush as we neared the home of the Grateful Dead. The group's leader, Jerry Garcia, was a folk hero to these devoted French students. They stood up and cheered when we reached the band's former Victorian home at 710 Ashbury Street.

There was also a round of applause for their spirited tour guide when they dropped me off downtown before returning to Oakland. Stopping by the office before going over to the Greyhound, I told the staff about my day—including my experience with the Hallidie Plaza rats. Someone suggested I phone Herb Caen and tell the local columnist my story—and I couldn't resist. Moments later I was on the phone with his office.

Several days later Herb Caen opened his August 18, 1977 column with a lengthy piece on the "Reverend" Jim Jones who had recently fled the city. Along with his usual array of news, views, and anecdotes, Caen mused on the recent death of Elvis Presley. Closing his column with characteristic wit and bite, he described my local encounter with the plaza rats. He set the stage with comments about what a great tourist month the city was having. He said the hotels were "jammed" so "who cares about dirty streets?" He wrote:

> MEANWHILE: It may come as a surprise that July was a bad month in the tourist biz, our biggest. Empty hotel rooms and half-filled restaurants inspired

emergency meetings among our touristic titans, some of them crying "Jail the freaks!", roust the sidewalk merchants and even clean the streets. However, August is a record-breaker. Hotels are jammed and who cares about dirty streets? ...Spinoff: At 5 a.m. a few mornings ago, Warren Smith, a social worker with Travelers Aid, started down the escalator steps into Hallidie Plaza, and recoiled in horror. "I had to fight my way through an army of about 40 rats, tearing at the garbage. I felt like I was in the middle of 'Willard.' A couple of dozen were near the Visitors Center chewing away." Since the rats weren't wearing badges, it is not believed they were convention delegates. Local rats.

People enjoyed Herb Caen's take on my early-morning adventure, and I received a number of "Way to go!" phone calls from friends and acquaintances the day the story ran. But late in the afternoon I had an angry call from one of the "touristic titans" at the San Francisco Chamber of Commerce. He said I did the city "a great disservice" by making the Hallidie rat incident such a public event. Why had I talked with Herb Caen? Where was my loyalty to San Francisco? What was I trying to accomplish?

But as he continued his diatribe, I suspected the real reason he was so upset was because the Chamber had been one of the *sponsors* of the brown-bag lunch event that had left such a mess in Hallidie Plaza—and Herb Caen's column had publicly embarrassed the organization for failing to clean up after itself. They were the ones, literally and figuratively, left holding the bags. After some further venting, the Chamber representative hung up in a huff.

For a few moments I was thrown by his call. Yet, as I thought about his anger toward me, I had to smile. It was obviously a lot easier to pick on a Travelers Aid social worker than the most popular newspaper columnist in the city of San Francisco. The Chamber of Commerce could try to make me the "rat" if they wanted, but one thing was for sure. Thanks to the Caen column, the San Francisco Chamber of Commerce would make sure that

Hallidie Plaza was as clean as a whistle after any future brown-bag lunch events. Herb Caen had done it again.

Given that hosting guided tours was not my usual practice, I was glad to get back to my regular duties helping troubled travelers. And while some travelers came from as far away as France, some came from just a mile or two away.

Pacific Heights Teenager

...for when I am weak, then I am strong.
—2 Corinthians 12:10

The twenty-two blocks from Pacific Heights to the Tenderloin is more than a long walk for a young teenager. It is a journey between two different worlds. Pacific Heights was the more secure and protected world of the middle and upper class, while the Tenderloin was home for many of the city's poorest and most underprivileged people.

Anna was only sixteen years old. She had a pug nose, brown eyes, and beautifully braided long blonde hair. Dressed in a fashionable skirt and sweater, she *looked* like a girl from Pacific Heights. Because Anna was a resident of San Francisco, she fell outside our normal Travelers Aid guidelines—as a rule we only served people who had been in San Francisco forty-five days or less. But there were times like this when we stretched our guidelines.

Frightened and confused, Anna was way over her head in the Tenderloin. Earlier that morning, she'd run away from home. It had been an impulsive move on her part, and as soon as she was on the streets she didn't know what to do. So she started walking and just kept on walking. After arriving downtown, she realized she hadn't thought things through. Although extremely unhappy at home, she was already wondering if she'd made a big mistake by running away. With tears rolling down her cheeks, she said she seemed to make a mess of everything—even running away.

She described how there was a real lack of communication in her family. Consumed with their jobs, her parents had no idea she was so depressed, and in her desperation she'd convinced herself that running away would solve her problems. But now the whole thing felt "stupid"—yet another one of her self-described failures. While completely out-of-sync with her parents, she made it clear that parental abuse was *not* a factor in her running away—she was just extremely depressed and lonely. Because she was already second-guessing her decision, I suggested she take another look at her situation before proceeding any further. I would help her explore her options if she was willing and she readily agreed.

First of all, I described a toll-free service called Peace of Mind. If she wanted, they would let her parents know she was all right but without disclosing her location. This might ease her parent's concern and minimize police involvement. I told her about Huckleberry House, the local runaway shelter. They could take her in, but because she was still a minor she would have to get her parent's permission to stay there—it was the law. I explained that would be the case at any type of shelter in any town, as well as for Travelers Aid. We could possibly house her temporarily, but we would need her parent's permission.

Continuing to lay out her options—including contacting Legal Services for Children and the National Runaway Switchboard—I mentioned that the Haight-Ashbury Switchboard might be able to find her a "crash pad" out in the Haight neighborhood near Golden Gate Park. The hip and savvy switchboard emerged during the Haight-Ashbury Summer of Love as a way to match stranded young people with sympathetic locals willing to house them on a short-term basis. But I warned that life on the run had become increasingly dangerous. The Haight's "peace, love, and happiness" days were short-lived and over. I warned her that many runaways bottom out on the streets of San Francisco.

After reviewing virtually every possible avenue of assistance, I gently reminded Anna she could also return home, and that doing so wouldn't have to signify a defeat on her part. However, if she chose to go back, it would be important to let her parents know how she was feeling. Perhaps some family counseling could improve their communication with one another.

Anna thanked me for listening and presenting her with various options. She would try to find a place where she could think things through. Before she left, I wrote down the phone numbers for the resources I'd discussed with her. I let her know I'd be at the Greyhound until ten that night if she still needed to talk, and she could always see one of our other social workers in the main office during the day.

An hour later, Anna called to tell me she was on her way home. Being on the streets had given her a much different perspective on her situation, and she knew that going home was the right thing to do. She would tell her parents she ran away, but only got as far as the Tenderloin before changing her mind. She would explain how unhappy she was and suggest they get some counseling together. Anna sounded relieved—and I was too. With her new resolve to clear the air with her parents, maybe things were about to get better for Anna and her family.

Just as returning home did not have to mean defeat for Anna, it did not have to mean defeat for Marge Henry either.

Chicago Mother

Discretion shall preserve thee, understanding shall keep thee.
—Proverbs 2:11

A middle-aged woman stepped up to the Travelers Aid booth with her three teenage boys and eight suitcases. Her name was Marge Henry and she and her sons had just arrived on a Greyhound bus from Chicago. Subdued, with an almost tragic air about her, she had dirty blonde hair and a slight southern accent. She was forty-seven years old.

Divorced ten years previous, she was bored with her job as a plater—she'd held that same position in the same factory for nearly twenty years. She was also tired of living in Chicago; the summers were hot, the winters brutally cold. Constantly depressed, exhausted by work, and worn down by family responsibilities, she would fall asleep every evening watching TV. Many nights she would cry herself to sleep. She did this day after day… week after week…year after year.

As far as her employer was concerned, Marge and her family were on a normal three-week vacation that would end with her return to work. But her "dream" was to find a job in San Francisco and *never* go back to Chicago and her monotonous job. She'd wanted to live in San Francisco for as long as she could remember and now she finally had her chance. The family brought all their clothing and personal belongings with them, but left their Chicago apartment furnishings intact—just in case. The rent was paid for the month, and if she couldn't find work they'd simply return home.

However, in talking with Marge it became obvious that she had done little or no planning in regard to their possible move. She asked my advice on everything—where to stay, where to seek employment, and what to do. Apparently she had been so depressed in Chicago that she waited until they arrived in San Francisco to figure things out.

To help conserve their money, I recommended they stay in a family room at the Coronado Hotel. The weekly rate at the Coronado was less than the daily rate at the more touristy hotels outside the Tenderloin. After reserving a room there at her request, I supplied her with maps, brochures, and other helpful information. I shared everything I knew about getting work and accessing community resources, and she said she would give it her all. If she found a job before the end of her "vacation," the family would remain in San Francisco. If not, they would go back to Chicago. It was as simple as that.

Two weeks later, a dejected Marge Henry and her boys came to our Travelers Aid booth. Things were not going well. She'd gone to various employment agencies, checked want ads, and made numerous phone calls, but nothing was available for someone with her limited experience. I tried to encourage her, but I knew that finding work in the city could be challenging. Marge said she would keep looking and hope for the best. She still had some time left.

The following week, Marge arrived at the Greyhound with her three boys and eight suitcases. They were taking the Greyhound back to Chicago. Try as she might, she had been unable to find a job. But to my surprise, she seemed strangely at peace about returning to a place she had previously described so negatively— and she told me why.

Several days before, while sitting around their hotel room, the family realized how homesick they were. After three weeks in the Bay Area they'd come to the sudden understanding that *Chicago*, not San Francisco, was their real home and where they wanted to be. Absence—along with Marge's inability to find a job—had literally made their hearts grow fonder.

Marge knew that when she returned to Chicago she'd have to be more patient at work. She'd also have to be more creative with her time off—there were definite things she would need to do to make their life more interesting and meaningful. But she already had a better attitude about her job at the factory. Not finding work in San Francisco made her appreciate the fact that she *had* a job in Chicago. Smiling at the thought, she said no one would ever have to know that her trip to San Francisco had been anything more than a family vacation.

While Marge regretted that so much of their time had been taken up by her job search, they had managed to have some real fun the last few days of their trip. The family had taken a cable car ride to Fisherman's Wharf, walked across the Golden Gate Bridge, rode the ferry to Sausalito, and enjoyed hot fudge sundaes at the Ghirardelli Chocolate Factory. Freed from the stresses of possible relocation, they'd all had a great time in the city. With a resigned smile, she said they hoped to return some day for a *real* vacation.

Like Marge, Joel was also from the Midwest and had trouble finding work in the city. But rather than returning home, he came up with another solution.

Joel

Therefore her young men shall fall in her streets...
—Jeremiah 49:26

Joel was eighteen years old, with blonde hair, blue eyes, and country good looks. Like Marge Henry and so many others, he'd always wanted to live in San Francisco and had hitchhiked out to California from his rural home in Iowa to make his dream come true. As we talked at the Travelers Aid booth, he said he was staying with some people he'd met on the street— not a great situation, but at least he had a place to sleep. After giving him some leads on employment, I handed him my card and told him to call me if he ran into trouble.

Several months later I was walking back on Market Street from the Greyhound to our main office. The summer fog was rolling over Twin Peaks as night descended on the city. A chilly wind accompanied the heavy mist and blew some papers along the sidewalk in front of me. On brisk nights like these I recalled the famous line attributed to Mark Twain: "The coldest winter I ever spent was a summer in San Francisco."

As I neared our office on Mason Street, I saw the usual group of young men gathered by the big plate glass window in front of the Flagg Brothers Shoe Store. This location was a popular pickup spot at night for "closeted" and older gay men willing to pay for young male hustlers. Under the orange glow of the city streetlights, they would cruise by the shoe store in their slow-moving automobiles. Hidden in the dark interiors of their cars, these faceless figures would periodically stop and negotiate with their potential partners through their barely opened car windows.

On this particular night, Joel was one of those standing in front of the shoe store. I was sorry to see him there, but it didn't come as a complete shock. It was all too common for young men like Joel to arrive in San Francisco with their California pipe dreams, only to end up on the street hustling to survive. A few of them eventually surfaced at the Greyhound hoping for a bus ticket home, some escaped to other parts of the city, while many just descended further and further into the depths of the Tenderloin.

I never saw Joel after that night at the shoe store. Maybe he kept working the streets. Maybe he found a job. Or maybe he went back to Iowa where the 4H clubs of his youth were a million miles away from the Tenderloin and the Flagg Brothers Shoe Store.

During this period of time in the late 1970s, large numbers of gay men were moving to San Francisco. Some like Joel were young without any specific job skills. Others like James Hardy had a solid work history—and even a wife and family.

The Hardy Family

Whereas ye know not what shall be on the morrow.

—James 4:14

In the 1970s San Francisco became a mecca for gays. At our Greyhound Travelers Aid booth we saw many gay men and women who'd left their conservative hometowns for the more liberal and accepting environment San Francisco provided them. Just as the Haight-Ashbury district was a magnet for hippies and "flower power" in the '60s, the Polk and Castro areas of San Francisco became a hub for homosexuals and "gay power" in the '70s.

San Francisco Chronicle reporter Randy Shilts, in his 1987 best-selling book about the AIDS epidemic titled *And the Band Played On*, described this influx of gays into the city:

> The promise of freedom had fueled the greatest exodus of immigrants to San Francisco since the Gold Rush. Between 1969 and 1973, at least 9,000 gay men moved to San Francisco, followed by 20,000 between 1974 and 1978. By 1980, about 5,000 homosexual men were moving to the Golden Gate every year. The immigration now made for a city in which two in five adult males were openly gay. (p.15)

In the midst of this gay influx, James Hardy stopped by the Travelers Aid booth one night to talk as he waited for his bus to the airport. Friendly and quick-witted, he was in his mid-to-late thirties. While he lived and worked in Chicago, business trips frequently brought him to San Francisco. He explained that although he was married and had two children, he was gay. He had hoped marriage would change his sexual orientation, but it didn't.

Speaking candidly, he described his recent involvement in the San Francisco gay community. On trips to the city, he was visiting leather bars, bathhouses, and even the infamous Jaguar Bookstore. While proud of his new anything-goes, "out of the closet" lifestyle, he had yet to tell his wife about his homosexuality—or about the San Francisco man he was getting involved with.

On a return trip several months later, James came by the Travelers Aid booth again. He'd accepted a sales position in San Francisco and he and his family would be moving to the city. His wife was still unaware of his secret life because he'd decided to wait until they'd moved before breaking the news—he was afraid she would remain in Chicago with the kids if he told her now. He said he *had* to be near his children. When I expressed my concern on how he was doing this, he replied "It's just the way it has to be."

When I saw James next, he and his family had moved to San Francisco. He said he was in the process of divorcing his wife and was already living with his new male partner. The children were doing "fine," but his wife was not; would I please talk with her? After giving me her number, I called and set up an appointment.

The next week I met with Susan Hardy in our office. She described her shock when James told her he was gay. She was trying to be understanding for the sake of the children, but she said she had some serious issues to work through. After providing some much-needed emotional support, I referred her to several community resources I thought would be helpful—including our Travelers Aid Tenderloin Childcare Center.

Located in the heart of the Tenderloin, our childcare center provided individual counseling and group support as well as crucial daycare services. It became a great resource for Susan and the children. Fortunately, she liked San Francisco and was determined to make things work for all of them.

Several months later the Hardy's divorce was finalized. They'd agreed to share custody of the children and the former couple not only remained friends, but were mutually supportive of each other's now very different lives.

When AIDS broke out in San Francisco a few years later, I thought of James and remembered his anything-goes attitude before moving in with his male partner. Hopefully, he and Susan and his partner escaped this disease that so many others did not.

And while sexual indiscretion was increasingly endangering people, both straight and gay, spiritual indiscretion was also taking its toll. Religious "cults" were gaining new members every day. Breaking away from these groups was often very difficult, but Tom was one of those who did.

The "Moonie"

Take heed that no man deceive you.

—Matthew 24:4

Tom was physically, mentally, and spiritually exhausted. The tall, blond-haired young man had hitchhiked in from Northern California. He had been living in Boonville in a religious commune devoted to the Reverend Sun Myung Moon—the controversial South Korean minister who headed the Unification Church and claimed to be the Messiah. Captivated by Moon's teachings, Tom had traveled to the church's Boonville training facility to get more deeply involved. But he quickly became disillusioned by the group that he was now calling a "cult." Describing the strict spiritual regimen that was enforced from early morning until late at night, he said he felt like he was being "brainwashed." When he started asking too many questions, the group turned on him and made it difficult for him to leave.

Finally fleeing the commune, he'd hitchhiked the hundred and ten miles from Boonville to San Francisco. Dropped off in San Francisco by his last ride, his plan was to spend the night in Golden Gate Park and in the morning hitchhike to Los Angeles, where he would stay with his brother. He had no intention of asking *anyone* for help—he'd gotten himself into this mess and he would get himself out. But then someone told him about Travelers Aid.

Concerned because Tom was so vulnerable and fatigued, I said we would be glad to provide him with food and a room for the night. I told him I was familiar with the "Moonies"—they often approached me on Market Street when I walked between our office and the Greyhound. Because I wore jeans, hiking boots, and carried a daypack, they assumed I was new in town and would be open to their overtures. Their come-on was a "free dinner" and "spiritual lecture" in the more upscale Pacific Heights part of the city. I knew their ultimate goal was to enlist new followers and to get them up to Boonville, just as they had with Tom.

Tom said he'd learned a hard lesson with the "Moonies" and was obviously relieved to be out of Boonville and away from the group. After providing emotional support and spending more than an hour with him, I gave him the necessary vouchers for food and lodging, along with directions to the Coronado Hotel. After thanking us for our help, he said he would be more careful in any future spiritual pursuits.

Later that evening, as I wrote up his case in our Mason Street office, I reflected on everything Tom had shared. It was inconceivable to me how a seemingly rational person like Tom could get so involved with a charismatic, guru-type spiritual figure like Sun Myung Moon. Little did I know then that just three years later—after I had left Travelers Aid and San Francisco—I would return to the city for a weekend celebration as a follower of Indian guru Bhagwan Shree Rajneesh. Dressed in all orange-dyed clothing, I would dance and meditate with a hundred other Rajneesh devotees in the basement of the First Congregational Church at the corner of Mason and Geary. Ironically, the church was just four blocks away from the Travelers Aid office where I had sat and wondered how anyone could get so involved with a charismatic, guru-type, spiritual figure like Sun Myung Moon. Ultimately, I would end up fleeing the Rajneesh movement, just as Tom fled from the "Moonies"—but that's another story and another book.

A further side note—because Travelers Aid networked with many other community resources, I'd become aware of a church in the city that was gaining a reputation for its "good works" by providing support services to low-income people. The charismatic minister was highly respected by many of San Francisco's political leaders. In fact, Mayor George Moscone appointed him to the San Francisco Housing Authority Commission and he later became the presiding chairman. This minister was none other than the infamous "Reverend" Jim Jones.

By 1977, there were growing reports of abuse regarding Jones and his People's Temple. In the midst of the breaking scandal, Jones and many in his congregation fled to their Guyana compound—commonly called "Jonestown"—that was located in the northeastern part of South America. In November 1978, Bay Area Congressman Leo Ryan and four others in Ryan's delegation to investigate Jonestown were murdered by People's Temple gunmen as they attempted to leave Guyana. Immediately following those murders, 900 of Jones' followers committed mass suicide or were murdered in their cult compound. Mayor George Moscone, who was previously supportive of Jones, would himself be shot and killed in an unrelated murder eight days later by a disgruntled former city supervisor named Dan White. White also murdered San Francisco supervisor Harvey Milk, the first openly gay man to be elected to public office in California. San Francisco and the world were rocked by these tragic events that ended one of the most violent decades in the city's history.

Looking back on the People's Temple now, it's hard to believe that Jim Jones had gained the respect of so many San Francisco leaders. It was yet another example of how the heads of certain churches and spiritual organizations can deceive not only individuals, but also whole communities through the smokescreen of their charitable good deeds. The People's Temple and their "good works" had provided a perfect cover for Jones until two persistent reporters from *New West Magazine* exposed the manipulation and abuse that was going on behind the scenes.

But while Jones and his church exploited people in the city, scores of other churches and faith-based charities were caring and helpful to those in need. St. Boniface Church fed people daily at St. Anthony's Dining Hall. Glide Church, Old St. Mary's Church, St. Patrick's Church, Raphael House, Salvation Army, San Francisco Gospel Mission, Lifeline Mission, the Night Minister, and many others provided essential services for homeless and low-income people.

I had often referred clients to these places, but it took a rainy-night encounter with a homeless man named Fred to get me to finally visit the two gospel missions.

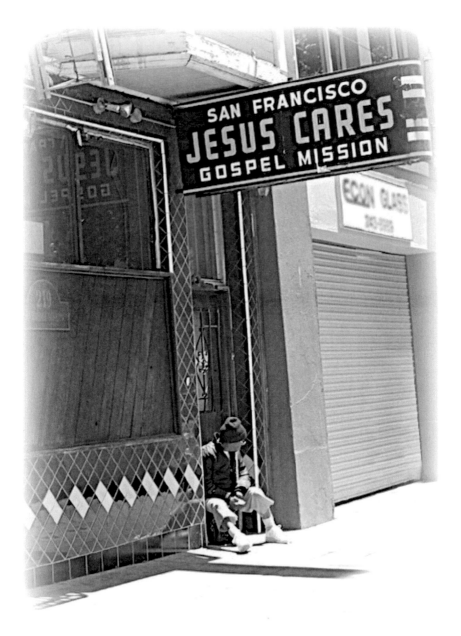

San Francisco Gospel Mission
219 Sixth Street
(Photo by Gloria Judd)

"Freight Train" Fred

Not that I speak in respect of want: for I have learned,
in whatsoever state I am, therewith to be content.

— Philippians 4:11

I will always remember him as "Freight Train" Fred. It was a wild, stormy night when he walked into the Greyhound as I was closing our booth for the evening. Tired and wet, he carried only a simple bedroll. The rain had flattened out his thin gray hair and his well-worn clothes were soaked. Seventy-three years old, and he was still riding the rails. He had just hopped off a freight train from Los Angeles and was looking for a place to spend the night.

He knew it was late, but asked if there were any beds still available at the missions. When I told him they were closed and probably full because of the rain, he wasn't surprised or even discouraged. He said he would find cover somewhere—he'd done it many times before. There were the building overhangs on Market Street and the tunnels on Folsom.

Travelers Aid wasn't set up to house lifestyle transients. We usually referred them to the rescue missions; if the missions were full, they were on their own. But on a whim, I called the San Francisco Gospel Mission. They had closed their doors several hours earlier, but it was worth a try. I was surprised when the woman at the mission said to send him right over. Fred and I were grateful they were bending their rules on this rainy night.

The city's two rescue missions had a reputation for being fairly regimented. Their hours and rules were very specific: People *had* to be there by a certain time, and they *had* to attend the evening service. There was some grumbling on the street about the rules and how you had to "sing for your supper," a derogatory reference to the mandatory hymn-singing and nightly church service that preceded getting a meal and a bed for the night. Many street people were upset with this "churchy" requirement.

I had always intended to visit the missions to learn more about them. Because the San Francisco Gospel Mission had been so kind to Fred, it seemed like a good time to check them out. The next evening, I walked the four long blocks from the Greyhound to the mission. Part of a large network of organizations that served people in the inner city, the Gospel Mission was located south of Market on Sixth Street in the heart of skid row, in what was cynically referred to as "the wine country." Turning the corner at Sixth Street, the sidewalk was teeming with groups of people smoking, drinking, and hanging out.

When I arrived at the mission, the front door was open. Inside the entryway a large placard was emblazoned with a verse from the Bible: "The wages of sin is death; but the gift of God is eternal life through Jesus Christ our Lord." Several Bibles and a number of pamphlets lay on a nearby table. In the main room to my left, thirty to forty men and women were sitting on couches and folding chairs, waiting for the evening service to begin. I looked around for the man who had inspired my visit, but "Freight Train" Fred was nowhere in sight—maybe he was already on another train to yet another town. But thanks to him, I'd finally made it to the mission.

Entering the room as discretely as possible, I sat down on one of the brown metal chairs and joined the group. No one said a word. The woman sitting on the couch in front of me had no shoes. A balding man in bib overalls sat alone in the corner. A young man with a ponytail and a beard was asleep to my left. As I sat there a peaceful calm seemed to envelop the room. The term "holy hush" came to mind and the depth of what I was feeling took me by surprise. No longer the curious social worker, I felt humbled to be with these people and in this place.

Moments later, five members of a black Baptist church from the city's Western Addition were introduced to everyone. Dressed impeccably, it was their night to do the service. The leader of the group greeted us warmly. His friendly, respectful manner appeared genuine. After a short prayer we sang a hymn and then another man from their group read from the Bible. It was the verse about perfect love casting out fear. I remember thinking that these church people seemed to really reflect the love of God they were talking about.

When the service was over, I felt extremely uplifted by what I had just experienced. As I walked back onto Sixth Street, skid row didn't seem so depressing and a brilliant orange-red sunset in the western sky seemed to magnify the deep feelings the service had inspired in me. This heightened state remained with me all the way back to the Greyhound. Because of this unexpectedly positive experience, I decided to go to the other rescue mission the next night.

The following evening, I stood in line outside the Lifeline Mission at Fifth and Folsom. Shortly before the mandated service, we were ushered into a side room that served as a chapel. After the director introduced himself, he told us they had a special guest speaker and that we were in for "a real treat." But when the speaker came out, I couldn't believe my eyes. It was Red, the controversial Market Street evangelist who was always telling everyone they were going to hell. And that was exactly what he told us that night—over and over and over again. His harsh sermon was quite a contrast to the loving one preached the previous night at the other mission.

To say the least, I was a bit confused as I walked back to the Greyhound after the service. The night before, I had felt so much love coming from those black Baptists. With Red it seemed just the opposite. It was hard to believe they shared the same Christian faith. In fact, Red seemed to reinforce the negative stereotype so many people had about street evangelists and rescue missions.

As a postscript to this story, in 2005 I returned as a committed Christian to that same San Francisco Gospel Mission I had visited twenty-eight years before. I was amazed when the person who greeted me at the door turned out to be JoAnn Knight, the very same woman who had made that rainy night exception for "Freight Train" Fred so many years ago. This dedicated lady and her husband were still working at the rescue mission.

I told her about my Travelers Aid experience with the two missions in the late '70s—how I'd enjoyed the black Baptists but had been turned off by Red's approach. I was taken aback when she told me that Red had preached at their mission too. I was *really* taken aback when she told me that he had actually helped a lot of people over the years. In fact, many folks had specifically asked for Red when they lay sick or dying at San Francisco General Hospital. She recounted how a number of men and women—even young people—had beaten drugs and alcohol and gotten off the streets because of his ministry. Red took a tough love approach to the Gospel, she said, but he had a heart for street people and a heart for the Lord.

I confided that I was surprised to hear all this. For years I'd been carrying a certain image of him around in my mind. Had I failed to see his sincerity and simply bought into the negative stereotype of a street evangelist? Was I so spiritually lost back in my Travelers Aid days that I missed the heart of who he was and what he was doing? Yet as I stood there thinking about all this, I had to be honest with myself. If I had been sick and dying in a San Francisco Hospital bed—with all due respect to the Market Street evangelist—I *still* would have called for those black Baptists and let old Red—God bless him—visit someone else.

With the holidays soon approaching, Tenderloin resources like the San Francisco Gospel Mission would be reaching out to people in a special way. Travelers Aid at the Greyhound would be no exception.

Christmas Eve at the Greyhound

And now abideth faith, hope, charity, these three;
but the greatest of these is charity.

—1 Corinthians 13:13

It was a chilly Christmas Eve as I made my way up Market Street toward the Greyhound. Last-minute shoppers boarded a Market Street trolley as local panhandlers made their final appeal for seasonal spare change. At the corner of Golden Gate and Market, a Salvation Army band did a nostalgic oom-pah-pah version of "Silent Night" in front of the Hibernia Bank. I stopped a moment and joined the crowd that had gathered. Hearing the familiar carol evoked a flood of memories from childhood Christmas's past: the holiday pageants at school, the Christmas Eve service at our New England Congregational Church, and my mother reading the Christmas story before we opened our presents. When the band went on to play "God Rest Ye Merry Gentleman," many of us sang along:

God rest ye merry gentleman, Let nothing you dismay,
Remember Christ our Saviour Was born on Christmas day,
To save us all from Satan's power; When we were gone astray.
O Tidings of comfort and joy, comfort and joy,
O Tidings of comfort and joy.

As I continued on to the bus station, I hoped Travelers Aid would extend some of that same "comfort and joy" to those needing help this night before Christmas. Entering the Greyhound and looking around the lobby, I couldn't imagine a more appropriate place to be on Christmas Eve. Travelers arriving in time for their

Christmas visits to local friends and family hurried through the lobby with their suitcases and presents. Outside, the cabs were doing a brisk business getting everyone to where they needed to go; inside, some of the Greyhound regulars had already arrived. They preferred to spend Christmas Eve in the busy bus station rather than their lonely hotel rooms.

Shortly after I'd opened the Travelers Aid booth, a young woman approached me sobbing hysterically. She'd arrived on a bus from Chicago, only to learn that her boyfriend had left town the day before with all their money. She was totally distraught because she had sent him her entire savings to put down on the apartment they were planning on renting together in San Francisco. Devastated, she was now stranded at the Greyhound with no boyfriend, no money, and no place to live.

With her permission, I called Raphael House and made arrangements for her to stay at their women's shelter throughout the holidays. I also gave her a referral to talk with one of our daytime social workers. Travelers Aid would try to assist her any way we could. If she wanted to return to Illinois, we would try to help her get back home. If she wanted to stay in San Francisco, we could help with that, too. After talking with her and providing some emotional support, I put her in a cab to Raphael House. One of their workers said the young woman would arrive just in time for their Christmas party. And while she might not feel particularly festive, at least she wouldn't be stranded at the Greyhound on Christmas Eve.

For the rest of the evening there was a steady stream of clients asking for various types of assistance. Some needed food and lodging; others simply wanted to talk. In one involved case, I worked with the Canadian Embassy to help two stranded Canadians return to Vancouver, British Columbia for a late Christmas with their families.

Before closing, a reporter from the *San Francisco Examiner* interviewed me for a story they were doing about people who were working on Christmas Eve. Without disclosing their identities, I described some of the people I had seen at our Travelers Aid booth. The next day—Christmas Day—the *Examiner* ran the Christmas

Eve article as a featured front-page story. Under the banner headline "Sniper eludes MPs in Presidio shootout" was the reporter's article about some of us who worked Christmas Eve. He described how the Christmas holiday might give the city some "much-needed time for warmth and relaxation" after "one of the most violent periods in San Francisco's history." Prior to the pre-dawn shootout at the Presidio military base, the reporter wrote how the streets had been "quiet" and for people who had to work, business was also for the most part "quiet."

He then described my busy evening at the Greyhound. He followed that with his account of others who had worked Christmas Eve, including a waitress at Henry Africa's restaurant, the night auditor at the Fairmont Hotel, and a doorman at a North Beach strip club.

Scattered throughout this Christmas edition of the *Examiner* were other holiday stories. One was about a thoroughbred horse named Santa Claus who won the third race at the New Orleans Fairgrounds the day before Christmas. Another article highlighted the pop music scene over the past year and featured a photo of Bob Dylan singing at the Winterland Ballroom. He had been a special guest at The Band's heavily publicized farewell concert, made famous in Martin Scorsese's film *The Last Waltz*. Dylan's short set included his song "Forever Young." And as I thought about it, the opening lines of that song perfectly expressed how I felt working at the Greyhound on Christmas Eve:

May God bless and keep you always
May your wishes all come true
May you always do for others
And let others do for you

And while Dylan captured the essence of giving and receiving in his inspirational song, so did the Bluesman one day at the Greyhound.

Passengers waiting in the Greyhound lobby
(Photo by Stephanie Maze)

The Bluesman

Break forth into joy, sing together...
—Isaiah 52:9

It was a rainy Saturday morning at the Greyhound. Not much was going on. Travelers waited patiently for the announcement that their buses were ready to board. Off to my right, several of the Greyhound regulars were drinking coffee and reading their papers—they were enjoying the anonymity and comfort of being around other people. Over towards the glass doorway leading to the departure gates, several people sat stone-faced watching the pay TVs that were attached to their bluish-gray fiberglass chairs. In the corner, a Market Street bag lady was hunched over in her seat sleeping soundly, all her worldly possessions in the large shopping bag by her side. It wouldn't be long before the security guard would spot her and ask her to leave. A couple seats down from her, a middle-aged man in a suit studied some papers he had just taken from his briefcase. It was unusually quiet in the Greyhound lobby—no street people, no drug deals going down, not even a passing drunk. Nothing much was happening at the Travelers Aid booth either. Tourists asked the usual questions about the city, but there'd been no crises and no real problems.

Gently floating into this rainy-day Greyhound collage was the sound of someone strumming a guitar. Near the cigarette machine, I saw an older black man sitting alone and playing his six-string. When he began to sing a blues number, several people turned their heads to listen. Moments later, he changed the tempo and sang a southern work song. Its playful melody and chorus were familiar to nearly everyone:

You got to jump down, turn around,
Pick a bale of cotton,
Got to jump down, turn around,
To pick a bale a day.

Many in the lobby were now looking over at the man and smiling. Some were even clapping their hands and joining in on the chorus. People who had been strangers a moment before were suddenly feeling more like family. The otherwise subdued Greyhound lobby had been magically transformed by the bluesman and a work song that Leadbelly once described as "this merry, swaggering song." Even the bag lady was now awake and taking it all in.

The music went on for a few more minutes—and then it was over. It must have been time for the old man's bus. He packed up his guitar and grabbed his suitcase. With a slight tip of the cap to his appreciative audience, he headed out to board his bus.

The lobby was still abuzz after the bluesman departed. But slowly, almost imperceptibly, many who had been relating to each other through his music were once again strangers. And as I looked around, I saw that most of the faces were no longer smiling. The Greyhound regulars had returned to their newspapers, people to their pay TVs, and over in the corner the bag lady was once again fast asleep.

Working for Travelers Aid was an incredible experience not just at Christmastime or when someone like the Bluesman lit up the lobby, but throughout the year. I often wished friends would come visit while I was working so they could see why I liked my job so much. One Saturday a friend of mine did visit, but things didn't turn out quite the way I had hoped.

My Friend the Photographer

...therefore shall ye flee...
—Isaiah 30:16

My Travelers Aid job often confounded my friends. While most of them worked nine-to-five Monday through Friday, my schedule included four nights a week and all day Saturday in the Greyhound bus station. When I would tell them how much I liked working at the depot and in the Tenderloin, they would scratch their heads in bewilderment—they assumed any job in the inner city would be depressing. I told them it was just the opposite. Being able to provide people with shelter, food, counseling, and appropriate referrals was a tremendous thing. Occasionally I invited my friends down to the Greyhound to visit. My neighbor Jan was one of the few who took me up on my offer.

Jan was a professional photographer who lived around the corner from me in the Bernal Heights section of the city. Curious about her work, I accompanied her once on a photo shoot. But while supportive of my Travelers Aid job, she was often puzzled by my enthusiasm. How could anyone *enjoy* working at the bus station? So one evening, as we caught up on what was going on in our lives, I invited her to come down one Saturday. It would give her a first-hand look at what I did and I could take her on a special tour of the Tenderloin.

She accepted my offer and we made plans for her to meet me at the Greyhound Travelers Aid booth the following Saturday. After spending some time at the bus station, I would show her several of the places I referred clients to—St. Anthony's Dining Hall, the San Francisco Gospel Mission, the Coronado Hotel—

and then we'd have lunch at a nearby café where the little jazz combo I liked so much often played. I was confident she would be inspired by the places she would see and the people she would meet—but that wasn't meant to be. In fact, Jan's trip to the Tenderloin started to short-circuit before she even entered the bus station.

The morning of her visit, a drunken man had walked in front of a Greyhound bus as it was making a wide right turn out of the depot. Medical personnel were on the scene when I arrived, but they had been unable to save him. There was still a lot of activity when Jan showed up half an hour later, and she was understandably upset about what had happened. Inside the Greyhound everyone was talking about the accident. We all felt bad for both the victim and the driver.

Obviously this wasn't the way I wanted to introduce Jan to the bus station and my job with Travelers Aid. I told her the incident was extremely unusual. Realizing it was best to get her away from the Greyhound and the accident aftermath, I suggested we head over to the San Francisco Gospel Mission. I wanted her to get a feel for what they did there, and while we walked I told her about "Freight Train" Fred and my recent visit to the mission.

As we approached the mission on Sixth Street, I noticed a man sitting on the sidewalk by the front door. He had an empty bottle in his right hand and seemed harmless enough just sitting there. However, as we neared the door, he started swearing profusely, his face red and contorted. Suddenly he smashed his bottle on the sidewalk right in front of us, sending shards of glass in every direction. Fortunately, neither of us was injured in the incident—but Jan was visibly shaken. Leading her quickly away from the man and the mission, I apologized and told her, once again, that this was a *most* unusual occurrence. Even with all of the drunks I encountered in the Tenderloin, no one had ever smashed a bottle in front of me like that.

Believing things could only get better, I walked Jan over to the café with the jazz combo I liked. I told her I especially enjoyed the saxophone player and how he seemed to spearhead the group. But when we arrived and sat down, I noticed the sax man wasn't with them. It was a real disappointment because I'd talked so enthusiastically about him to Jan.

At the end of the set, one of the band members stepped forward and told us why the saxophone player was absent—he'd been shot several days before. We were both horrified, and I wasn't surprised when Jan rose from her chair and said she had to go home. Her day in the Tenderloin was over—she wasn't about to wait around to see what would happen next. I walked her back to where she'd parked her car and then, still trying to comprehend the sequence of events that had just transpired, watched her drive away.

I called Jan the next day to see how she was doing. She said that when she returned from our "Tenderloin tour" she was so emotionally drained she'd taken a six-hour nap. Nonetheless, she thanked me for *trying* to show her around. She was glad people like me were willing to work in the inner city—but added that if she had her way, she would never, ever, go down there again.

But as one friend departed the Greyhound, a new special friend was arriving. Her name was Kari.

Kari

To every thing there is a season,
and a time to every purpose under the heaven...

—Ecclesiastes 3:1

It was a challenging time in my personal life. I had recently separated from Anne, the woman I'd been with the previous four years. Our closeness made letting go difficult for both of us. She had been such an integral part of my life. We would continue to be friends but a committed, long-term relationship was not to be. She had been so supportive as I tried to pull my life together after arriving in San Francisco. She was with me when I first volunteered at Travelers Aid and she was with me when I was hired as a Travelers Aid social worker. This former flight attendant with curly red hair, freckles, and a great smile, would go on to become a successful lawyer in Alaska, happily married to a man that she met in law school. I will be forever grateful for the time Anne and I had together. Several months after our parting, I met Kari.

Standing at the Travelers Aid booth one Saturday afternoon, I noticed the beseeching eyes of a young woman seated off to my right. Two local hustlers were pressuring her and trying to engage her in conversation. Smiling sweetly, yet looking over at me in utter exasperation, she seemed to be saying, "Could you *please* get these guys out of here?"

Walking over to where she was sitting, I greeted her as one would a friend—and the two street people quickly backed off and left. I introduced myself as the social worker for Travelers Aid and apologized for what had just happened. I told her that the Greyhound was a popular spot for people on the make; it was just the nature of the place.

She thanked me and told me her name was Kari. She'd just arrived on the local bus from Mountain View and was waiting for her sister to pick her up. Kari had dark hair, pretty eyes, light-brown skin, and a smile that never seemed to leave her face. I wanted to talk more, but I had to get back to work. I told her to come over to our booth if there was any further trouble.

Returning to the Travelers Aid counter, I would occasionally look her way. When I did, she would be looking at me and smiling. And while I knew something was happening between us, I also knew Travelers Aid wasn't paying me to meet women in the Greyhound lobby. But as the minutes passed by, all I could think of was her sister arriving—and my never seeing her again.

To keep from second-guessing myself later, I walked back to where Kari was sitting. Stammering slightly, I asked if I could call her sometime. Seemingly pleased, she wrote down her phone number and handed it to me. I told her I would be calling and then quickly doubled back to our booth where a small crowd had gathered. When I glanced over a short time later, she was gone. Her sister must have picked her up while I was helping someone. The lobby seemed empty without her.

I wasted no time in calling Kari. After our first date we were almost inseparable—except for a vacation I had already planned in the great Southwest.

Travelers Aid for Me

Trust ye not in a friend, put ye not confidence in a guide...
—Micah 7:5

It seemed so ironic to be going out with someone I met at the Greyhound bus station. Kari was living south of the city in Los Altos, but that didn't stop me from seeing her as often as I could. However, prior to meeting her I had already planned an extensive one-month vacation of driving, camping, and backpacking in the American Southwest, traveling to various national parks and historical landmarks related to Native Americans. Given her job and college studies, there was no way Kari could make the trip with me. So when the time came, I said good-bye to her and the Bay Area and headed off to Arizona. It would be good to get away from the city for a while.

After hiking and camping in the Havasupai Indian Reservation and in the main part of the Grand Canyon, I was one week into my vacation. Leaving the Grand Canyon area, it was on to new adventures as I drove deep into Navajo country. The high point of my trip would be a visit to the Pueblo ruins in Canyon de Chelly near the town of Chinle in northern Arizona. I also planned to visit the Mesa Verde National Park in Colorado before driving back home.

Canyon de Chelly National Monument is a beautiful historic area located within the 25,000 square mile Navajo Reservation (Navajo Nation) in the Four Corners area of remote northeastern Arizona. Still home to about thirty Navajo families in the summer months, Canyon de Chelly has been inhabited for some five thousand years; Navajos settled in the area in the late 1700s.

The ancient Anasazi cave and cliff dwelling ruins are the primary attraction for tourists who venture down into the twenty-seven-mile-long canyon. Tourists travel into the canyon on a large motorized vehicle operated by the National Park Service or by arranging a walking tour with one of the Navajo guides.

The sheer beauty of Canyon de Chelly was overwhelming. Inspired by the towering cliffs and ancient Indian dwellings I had seen on the motorized tour, I was determined to return to the canyon on foot. When I asked the tour driver how to arrange a walking tour, he referred me to a native guide named Alvin. An hour later, I found him by the park headquarters. The young Navajo had long, jet-black hair bound by a bright red bandana. He was wearing a yellow T-shirt, faded blue jeans, and a pair of running shoes. With his chiseled Navajo features, it didn't surprise me that his photograph had been included in a recent *Arizona Highways Magazine* devoted to Canyon de Chelly.

Charismatic and confident, Alvin was hip almost to the point of being cocky. He worked as a canyon guide during the tourist season but lived in Los Angeles during the winter months. Eager to accommodate me, Alvin said if I found eight other people willing to pay fifteen dollars apiece, he would take our group into a scenic side canyon where he and his sheep-herding father lived. He would show us rarely visited ruins and let us camp beside his family's traditional wooden Navajo dwelling, or "hogan."

Alvin explained that he and his father lived in Canyon del Muerto, another canyon that runs right alongside Canyon de Chelly. Named after a Spanish military expedition that murdered nearly one hundred Navajos in 1805, this "canyon of the dead" was also where Kit Carson and his troops captured countless Navajos back in 1864. Carson's campaign ultimately ended with the famous "Long Walk" of the Navajos to Fort Sumner in eastern New Mexico. Alvin promised he would take us to places that few white men had ever visited.

Excited by this unique opportunity, I walked around the campground recruiting people. Within twenty minutes I found eight other hikers who were interested. Our diverse group included a Purple Heart Vietnam veteran, a New York photographer, and a naturopathic physician from Santa Fe, New Mexico.

The following morning Alvin met us at the campground and directed us to an isolated area overlooking Canyon del Muerto. After we parked our cars near the edge of the cliff, he led us down a steep, unmarked trail into the heart of the canyon. While we cautiously navigated treacherous ledges in our sturdy hiking boots, Alvin scampered ahead in his running shoes. Following the challenging one-thousand-foot descent to the valley floor, we walked another mile or so until we arrived at Alvin's secluded hogan.

Awed by the utter beauty that surrounded us, we took short walks, read, relaxed, and settled in. That night, following a simple supper cooked outside, we all sat by the campfire with Alvin and his father. A full moon highlighted the canyon walls around us. "Oh, there's George Washington," Alvin's father declared as he gestured toward a particular rock formation across the way. Sure enough, it *really did* look like George Washington. He and Alvin went on to point out other canyon configurations that resembled famous people and familiar objects. Sitting by the campfire night after night for so many years, they'd probably discerned everything there was to discern from the cliffs that surrounded them. Later, after more stories around the campfire, we laid out our sleeping bags and slept peacefully under the starry night sky.

The next day Alvin led us to several Pueblo ruins in the immediate area. Some of the caves still contained ancient pottery fragments and centuries-old kernels of corn. Along the sweeping expanse of the canyon floor, other hogans were separated by many acres of land. Framed by the rugged canyon walls, enormous billowy white clouds, and a deep blue sky, this remote area was breathtaking. We saw very few Navajos—just two lone women harvesting plants for the colorful dyes they used in weaving. Sitting around the campfire that night, our little group agreed it had been an extraordinary day.

On our second full day in the canyon, we were more on our own. In the afternoon Alvin and I visited more Pueblo ruins.

A sign at one site prohibited entry and warned trespassers they would fall under a Navajo curse. Paying no attention to the sign, Alvin walked right in and motioned for me to follow. Because he was the official Navajo guide, I assumed it was all right for us to disregard the sign. Later, after further hiking and exploring, we returned in time for dinner and another night under the stars.

The next morning, as we all prepared to hike out of the canyon, Alvin took me aside and invited me to stay on at their hogan for another day or two. He explained that after taking the rest of the group to their cars, he was to lead a Sierra Club tour in the afternoon, then spend the night up top and hike back the next day. His father was already off to herd sheep and would also be away overnight, so I would have the whole area to myself until they both returned the next day.

Flattered by his invitation, I was happy to stay on. Before leaving with the group, Alvin asked if I was concerned about my car being parked so close to the canyon rim; if it made me feel more comfortable, he would move it back a bit. Because it seemed like a good idea, I gave him the keys to my car.

After saying good-bye to everyone, I spent a quiet day alone in beautiful Canyon del Muerto. But even amidst the picturesque surroundings, there was a subtle, surreal quality to what I experienced. It didn't escape me that I was in an area where white men had created so much misery and heartbreak for the Navajos, and as evening came on I felt somewhat uneasy. Thankfully, Alvin's dog was there to keep me company, sleeping by my side throughout the night.

Late the next afternoon, Alvin's father came back from herding sheep. Alvin hadn't returned yet, so it was just the two of us for dinner—fried potatoes under another spectacular evening sky. As we sat by the fire, his father suddenly exclaimed, "Oh, I wonder where Alvin is?" I explained that he'd led a Sierra Club tour, but was supposed to be back by now. I also mentioned that I'd given him the keys to my car so he could move it away from the edge of the canyon. "Oh, I would not have done that," was his father's instant reply. It was in that moment I realized I had made a big mistake in trusting Alvin with my car.

When Alvin didn't show up the next morning, his father and I hiked up an alternate trail to where the elder Navajo's truck was parked. It was a different area from where I had left my car. We'd driven only a short distance when we saw Alvin walking along the road. When we stopped I immediately asked him about my car, and to my relief he said that everything was fine. After a few words with his father, we headed out on foot to get my vehicle. But the moment his father drove away, Alvin turned to me and said, "I'm sorry, but I wrecked your car."

I exclaimed, "You *what?*"

Very matter-of-factly he said it again. "I wrecked your car."

When I asked him *how* he wrecked my car, he told me that he and a friend had been drinking and got into a fight.

"While you were driving my car you got into a fight?" I couldn't believe it. He attempted to reassure me by telling me he'd had it towed to the local body shop and they *might* be able to fix it.

Later, at the auto shop, the owner told me he needed to order parts and that it would take up to a week to *possibly* get the car running again. Despite the high estimate, I told him to go ahead and try to fix it. Now, with mounting expenses and a vacation that was quickly turning into a nightmare, I needed an inexpensive place to stay while my car was being repaired. With no car to secure my sleeping bag and belongings during the day, camping was out. But then Alvin said he knew the perfect spot—it offered free lodging and meals, and was within walking distance. Upon further inquiry, I learned that it was a local rescue mission run by the Presbyterian Church. Stunned by this turn of events but desperately needing to conserve my money, I reluctantly agreed to go there.

Alvin walked me over to the mission and introduced me to the minister who oversaw the mission. After being assigned a bunk and bidding good-bye to Alvin—whom I never saw again—I took a much-needed shower. The irony of my situation did not escape me. I was on vacation from my Travelers Aid job of helping travelers in trouble and I often referred people to rescue missions. Now here I was—a traveler in trouble, staying in a rescue mission. It was unbelievable. I had just become my own Travelers Aid case.

That night as we sang hymns at the evening church service, my situation felt like a huge cosmic joke—the vacationing Travelers Aid social worker "singing for his supper" in a rescue mission. But, truth be known, I was grateful for the free food and shelter. With a steep impending repair bill, it would have been very expensive staying in a motel for a week. That night as I slept at the mission with the local homeless, I was right where I needed to be.

After breakfast the next morning, I happened to walk by the office for Navajo Legal Services. Striking up a conversation with several of the workers, I told them about Alvin and what happened to my car. They could hardly keep from laughing. From their perspective it was probably a case of what goes around comes around for Mr. White Man.

That afternoon I went out on a work crew with some of the men staying at the mission. We did various odd jobs around the reservation. Though I was glad to help out, the thrill of my Native American vacation was rapidly fading. Maybe there *was* something to that curse Alvin and I had disregarded by entering that forbidden ruin.

At the end of the week, I was notified that my car had been repaired. I thanked the minister and his wife for their hospitality, then walked over to the auto shop and paid the high repair bill. I was more than ready to leave Canyon de Chelly and my car troubles behind. Driving out of Chinle toward Colorado and the Mesa Verde ruins, I hoped to redeem what was left of my sputtering vacation.

Near the outskirts of town, I picked up an elderly Navajo woman in a purple calico dress who was hitchhiking by the side of the road. As I drove on, it felt like the car was wobbling a bit from side to side. After dropping the woman off at her destination, the situation only got worse. Somehow I made it to a trading post that seemed to be in the middle of nowhere. As I pulled into the parking lot, my engine suddenly died. And when I got out of the car, I noticed that my two back wheels looked like they were about to fall off.

Inside the trading post, I was in the process of calling AAA for help when two salesmen walked through the door. Pointing to my broken-down VW in the parking lot, I said I would sell it lock, stock, and barrel for $250 and a ride into civilization—wherever that might be. I told them I'd paid a whole lot more than that to a mechanic earlier in the day, and nearly that amount for the four new tires I purchased prior to my trip. One of the men took me up on my offer and wrote me a check on the spot. He would have the car towed to a repair shop and completely overhauled for his daughter. After I removed my belongings and handed over the pink slip, he drove me to his home in Farmington, New Mexico, an hour or so away.

As I sat in his living room looking out at the southwestern sky, it hit me. My vacation was over. I had dead-ended in the Arizona and New Mexico deserts. There was nothing left to do but to call American Airlines and book a flight home for the following day. I spent the night at the salesman's house and the next morning he drove me to the Farmington Airport where I boarded my plane. Kari met me when I arrived in San Francisco and two days later I was back at work helping travelers in trouble.

And while a drunken tour guide had left me high and dry, a Bay Area housewife was left high and dry by her drunken husband.

The Tiburon Housewife

He that is soon angry dealeth foolishly...
—Proverbs 14:17

Late one Saturday afternoon at the Greyhound, a well-dressed, middle-aged woman approached the Travelers Aid booth. She lived in Tiburon, a picturesque upscale town across the Golden Gate Bridge in Marin County. Obviously embarrassed, she said she was out of money and trying to get home.

She and her husband had traveled to the seaside town of Carmel and stayed at a local inn for several days. Early that morning before checking out, her husband continued his drinking from the night before and became argumentative. Getting increasingly agitated, and after a particularly angry outburst, he stormed out of the room and drove off. He had all of their credit cards and most of their money—and didn't return. She said it was not the first time that he'd done this.

Fortunately, they'd already paid for their room, but she had to leave at checkout time and had only enough money to buy a bus ticket from Carmel to San Francisco. Distraught and apologetic, she asked if Travelers Aid could loan her the money she needed to take the Golden Gate Transit bus to Tiburon.

She was greatly relieved when I gave her money for the ticket and she left to catch her bus on Market Street. Soon afterwards we received a nice thank-you card and a generous donation that far exceeded the cost of her ticket.

The Tiburon housewife was fortunate that she had a home to return to. But when Stanley Baker's "friends" kicked him out of the flat they were sharing, he had nowhere to go but the street.

Warren Smith answering a page.
(Photo by John O'Hara)

Stanley Baker

And be ye kind one to another...
—Ephesians 4:32

I was paged late one night while walking through the Tenderloin. Stepping into a nearby phone booth, I called our answering service and was patched through to a man named Stanley Baker. He had recently arrived in San Francisco but had been kicked out of the flat where he was living with two other people. Because he was calling from a pay phone near the Coronado Hotel and sounded so depressed, I asked him to meet me at the hotel. When I got there I found him sitting on the front steps.

Stanley was a tall, effeminate, twenty-six-year-old black transsexual from Alabama who spoke with a slow southern drawl. His hair was pulled back in a matronly bun and his right hand was slightly deformed. His noticeably enlarged breasts were the result of hormone treatments started in Alabama. Stanley had always wanted to be a woman and hoped to have an operation that would complete the sex-change process, a procedure that a number of Tenderloin transsexuals had already undergone.

Life back in Alabama had been difficult. His mother was very loving, but his stepfather was not. His crippled hand was the result of childhood physical abuse by his stepfather. Stanley fled Alabama with two "friends" and they'd been in San Francisco for a month. The three of them had rented a flat in the Western Addition, but after a violent argument earlier in the evening, he'd been forced to leave and told never to come back. Now he was homeless with nowhere to go. His mother was willing to send him a bus ticket back to Alabama, but he wasn't sure he wanted to do that.

To meet his immediate needs for food and shelter, I housed Stanley at the Coronado for three nights and gave him several food vouchers. I also referred him to the Center for Special Problems (CSP). The Center had doctors, social workers, and counselors on staff who would try to assist him and provide emotional support.

Two days later I received a call from Stanley. He was in the psychiatric ward at San Francisco General Hospital after overdosing the previous day at the Center for Special Problems. It seemed that the CSP psychiatrist had only spent a couple of minutes with him before writing a prescription and moving on to the next patient. Feeling rejected and depressed, Stanley swallowed *all* the prescribed medication he'd just picked up at the CSP pharmacy. He collapsed on the spot and was rushed to San Francisco General. Stanley was calling me because the hospital wanted to release him but needed to know if he still had a room at the Coronado Hotel. I told him he did, and that I would immediately notify the discharge planner. I asked him to see me the next day at our main office.

Troubled by Stanley's account, I contacted a CSP social worker—and she confirmed Stanley's story. The psychiatrist had been far too brief with him and there had been no follow-up by their counseling staff. If Stanley was willing to return to CSP, she would personally handle his case and provide ongoing support.

Stanley came to see me the next day, accompanied by a transvestite friend named "Henrietta," and told me that he'd decided to remain in San Francisco. I explained that if he stayed in the city, he would need to move from our temporary room at the Coronado to a more permanent place. The best way for him to do this was to go to the Department of Social Services and apply for General Assistance (GA)—it would provide him with a week-to-week room in an inexpensive Tenderloin hotel, some food stamps, and medical coverage. He could remain at the Coronado until he was approved for GA. During our visit I shared my conversation with the CSP social worker, encouraging Stanley to see her and to give the center another chance. He said he would.

The following week, Stanley phoned to let me know he'd been approved for General Assistance and was now living at the Turk Street Hotel, just two blocks from our office. He had also seen the CSP social worker—but despite her support he was still very down.

Just *how* down became clear when I stopped by his hotel room a few days later. He was so depressed he could barely speak, and when he did it was only in a whisper. Even worse, he said he was having blackouts and losing track of time. After listening at length and trying to encourage him, I told him I would be back in the morning.

His depression was even more pronounced when I saw him the next day. With tears streaming down his face, he told me his dead brother was telling him to kill himself—that Stanley would find great peace on "the other side." While he was talking, I noticed the wire hangers that were attached to the light fixture on the ceiling. When I asked him about it, he said he was going to hang himself. He'd already tested it by standing on a chair and putting his head in the wire noose.

It was obvious Stanley needed to be readmitted to San Francisco General Hospital. When I told him I would accompany him there, he agreed to go and within ten minutes we were in a cab and on our way to the hospital. With his recent overdose, blackouts, hallucinations, suicidal thoughts, and the noose in his hotel room, I was sure the hospital would admit him. Clearly, he met the criteria of being a danger to himself.

At the hospital, the emergency room psychiatrist met with Stanley for about twenty minutes before meeting with me alone. I was dumbfounded when the doctor said he was *not* going to hospitalize him because he didn't believe Stanley was in immediate danger of killing himself. Thrown by his assessment, I went back over everything that had been happening, including Stanley's "conversations" with the dead brother and the noose in his hotel room. The doctor said he was aware of all that, but he couldn't admit him because he hadn't actually *tried* to kill himself. I urged him to reconsider, but he was firm in his decision.

During the subdued cab ride back to his hotel, I tried to explain to Stanley why he hadn't been admitted to the hospital—but the truth was I could hardly explain it to myself. Attempting to give him some kind of reassurance, I reminded him of his upcoming appointment with the CSP social worker and said we'd all continue to support him in every way possible. When we reached the hotel, I walked him to his room and spent another hour or so with him. Before leaving, I told him I would continue to visit, but needed him to promise that he wouldn't try to kill himself. He reluctantly agreed.

Everything came to a head the following Saturday. When I saw Stanley in the early afternoon he was in bed. His dead brother was still telling him to kill himself—and Stanley wanted to "be with him." At this point there was no way I could leave him alone—he obviously needed psychiatric care in a supervised setting. But given the hospital's recent refusal to admit him, I wasn't sure what to do. I decided to call the crisis line at the Tenderloin Clinic to enlist their help.

Reaching their weekend answering service, I was surprised when they patched me through to the director of the clinic. I told him I was convinced that Stanley was highly suicidal and that San Francisco General was refusing to admit him. I gave him all the facts and—thank God—he heard me.

On what was supposed to be his day off, the director immediately drove to the hotel to meet with Stanley and me. He was extremely compassionate and supportive and agreed with my assessment. He told Stanley he deserved to be getting proper treatment and that he would do everything he could to get him admitted to the hospital. After Stanley signed a consent form, the three of us were off to San Francisco General in the director's old red Volvo.

Within thirty minutes of our arrival, Stanley was admitted to the psychiatric unit. The director knew the psychiatrist on duty and this paved the way for his admission. Stanley would finally get some help.

Stanley responded well to his treatment. He was put on a new medication that helped relieve some of his depression, and he continued to see the CSP social worker after his release. Because the kind-hearted director put more value in Stanley's well-being than he did in enjoying his day off, Stanley was alive and had a new lease on life.

While Stanley *almost* fell through the cracks of the system, Lois Edwards *did* fall through the cracks—and it cost her dearly.

Lois

*For my soul is full of troubles: and my life
draweth nigh unto the grave.*

—Psalm 88:3

No doubt about it—the woman had suffered greatly. The lines on her face suggested she'd seen some very hard times: Her short brown hair needed washing, her eyes were dull, and her rumpled clothes looked like they'd been worn for days. Tall, thin, and pale, Lois Edwards appeared much older than the thirty-three years she wrote on her Travelers Aid application for assistance. I saw her late one Friday afternoon just after she had gone to the Department of Social Services (DSS), where she'd learned that their intake unit was closed until Monday. Speaking in a flat monotone, Lois said she had recently been hospitalized in nearby Marin County and was without any money or shelter. A worker at DSS told her about Travelers Aid.

Sensing something was terribly wrong, I asked Lois if I could speak with someone at the hospital where she had been treated in Marin. She gave me the number and sat quietly as I talked with a nurse familiar with her case, who told me that Lois had left their facility against medical advice. There had been no way of detaining her because there had been no commitment order. Diagnosed with severe depression, Lois needed to be taking the prescribed medication that had been helping her. The nurse hoped I could convince Lois to return to their hospital or go to some kind of in-patient treatment in San Francisco.

When I told Lois that the nurse had recommended she resume taking her meds and return to the hospital, she insisted she was fine—she didn't need any medication and wouldn't go back to the hospital. Trying to work around her obvious denial, I knew it was important to get her off the streets. I told her Travelers Aid would house her for the weekend at the Coronado Hotel and provide her with food vouchers, but stressed the importance of her returning to the Department of Social Services on Monday. She would surely qualify for its General Assistance program, which would provide emergency food stamps and enable her to get into longer-term housing.

To make things as smooth as possible, I called the Department of Social Services to let them know we were working with Lois. In addition, I wrote a detailed letter of referral to give to the intake worker. I also gave Lois my business card and a toll-free number for the Tenderloin Clinic crisis line. I told her I wouldn't be back to work until Tuesday, but she could see any of our other social workers on Monday if she had any problems at DSS.

Arriving at work on Tuesday, I learned there had been no contact from Lois and that she'd vacated her room at the Coronado Hotel. A call to the Department of Social Services revealed she hadn't gone to their offices either. For all intents and purposes, she had disappeared.

The following week I received a phone call from Lorenzo Dill, a psychologist at the Tenderloin Clinic. Their crisis line had just received a frantic call from a man living at the Coronado Hotel who was extremely concerned because a woman staying with him was threatening to jump out his third-story window. Her name was Lois and she had a Travelers Aid business card with my name on it. After sharing what little I knew about her, I agreed to meet Lorenzo in front of the Coronado and make a joint visit to see what we could do to help her.

Lorenzo and I spoke briefly on the front steps of the hotel, then went upstairs to see Lois. In the hallway, we met the man who'd called the crisis line. Lois had told him she was homeless and had nowhere to go; feeling sorry for her, he let her move in with him. But his compassion quickly changed to concern as he watched her sit on her bed for long stretches of time, staring into space, and then periodically hitting her head against the window frame and threatening to jump out. He became further alarmed when he discovered she had rat poison in her purse.

Entering the room, we found Lois sitting on the edge of her bed with a vacant look in her eyes. When Lorenzo introduced himself and asked how she was doing, she whispered, "Fine." As he gently questioned her about the rat poison and hitting her head against the window, she kept reiterating she was "fine." Getting right to the point, he asked if she was willing to see a doctor—and she flatly refused.

After conferring with Lorenzo in the hallway, we agreed that Lois *definitely* needed to be hospitalized. Because she wouldn't go voluntarily, we'd have to call the police and invoke a "5150" commitment order. The number referred to a section in the legal code authorizing involuntary hospitalization for someone who was a danger to themselves or others. Lois was clearly a danger to herself, and we knew that a 5150 might save her life.

Lorenzo drew up the necessary papers and called the police. As we waited for them to arrive, we explained our concern to Lois, and that we were sending her to the hospital to get some help. It was clear that she didn't want to go, but was too depressed to offer any real resistance. I then went downstairs and let Mr. Patel know what was happening.

When the police came, Lorenzo handed them the 5150 papers. After they left with Lois, Lorenzo phoned the hospital's psychiatric ward to give them a complete heads-up. Even though everything was detailed in the papers, he wanted to make sure they understood the gravity of her situation.

According to Lorenzo, the 5150 procedure was usually routine. The police would take Lois to the hospital's psychiatric unit and leave the commitment papers for the intake nurse who would then process her admission. While the hospital usually rubber-stamped his 5150s, Lorenzo had called ahead to make sure there wouldn't be any problems.

Walking back to the office, I was relieved that Lois would be back in a protective setting where she could get help for her depression. Although involuntary commitment orders can be controversial, I knew without a doubt that Lois needed to be hospitalized for her own safety.

The next day when I reported to work, I was told to call Lorenzo Dill immediately. When I phoned, he made sure I was alone in my office and sitting down. He then proceeded to tell me the tragic news.

"Warren, things went terribly wrong at the hospital yesterday. Lois was never admitted. After leaving the hospital, she went back to the Coronado Hotel and killed herself."

I sat in shocked disbelief as Lorenzo described the series of mishaps that occurred at the hospital. He said that when the police brought Lois in, there was a new intake nurse on duty. Inexplicably, she forgot to check the intake box where the police always put their 5150 papers—a mandatory and vital part of her routine. Compounding the problem, Lorenzo's call to the psychiatric unit hadn't been passed along to the intake nurse either, so she never knew the actual circumstances of why Lois was there. Lois, of course, told the nurse she was "fine" and that she didn't need any help.

Accepting Lois's statement as fact, the intake nurse wrongly assessed that what Lois *really* needed was a job. Her solution was to refer Lois to a job-training program and send her on her way. Lois then walked back to the Coronado to the man's room where she'd been staying. Later that night while he was sleeping, she swallowed a bottle of pills she had apparently hidden in the room.

Lorenzo said the new intake nurse had erred in almost every conceivable way. Everything that could possibly go wrong *had* gone wrong. Stunned by his account, I told Lorenzo how sorry I was. I said I needed time to process everything, but would be in touch.

Hanging up the phone, I sat at my desk trying to make sense of what happened. My feelings shifted back and forth between sadness and anger. The 5150 should have been a fairly simple procedure but bungling and miscommunication had turned it into an unnecessary tragedy. I felt sorry for Lois. I felt sorry for the man at the Coronado Hotel who tried to help her. And, when I allowed myself, I even felt sorry for the intake nurse—she had to be carrying quite a burden.

Every story does not have a happy ending, and it's hard to find any kind of silver lining in Lois' story. However, the next day the Director of Travelers Aid sent a letter to the head of the San Francisco Health Department. She documented the hospital's tragic mistakes regarding Lois and expressed her deep concerns about their 5150 intake procedures. Within a week, San Francisco General Hospital had completely revamped their 5150 policies. New protocols were instituted with checks and balances aimed to ensure that the errors made with Lois would never happen again.

In Lois's case, a woman who desperately needed to be *admitted* to a hospital had not been admitted due to procedural errors. In another Travelers Aid case, two young boys who desperately needed to be *released* from a hospital had not been released due to procedural errors.

Lenny and Ronnie

...knock, and it shall be opened unto you.

—Luke 11:9

"Hey Mister, we want a job." The brown-haired boy standing in front of the Travelers Aid booth blurted out his request in a halting yet determined manner.

His skinny, blond-haired friend quickly chimed in, "Yeah, we need a job." Neither of the boys looked a day over fourteen.

"How old are you?" I asked.

"Eighteen," said the first boy, squirming uncomfortably and avoiding any direct eye contact with me.

"Yeah, eighteen," stated the second one just as unconvincingly.

They told me they were best friends—"blood brothers"—and they needed work so they could get an apartment. Their attempt to present themselves as job seekers might have been humorous except for the fact that they were in the Greyhound bus station with no parent or accompanying adult in sight. The boys were putting on a brave front, but they were obviously nervous and not very good at lying. They were like ducks out of water at the depot, and I felt immediately protective toward them. When I asked if they were with anyone, they insisted they were on their own.

While the boys were noticeably naïve, there was a tenacious aspect to their boyish bravado—and it made my mind race with questions. What had brought them to the Greyhound? Had they run away from home or some kind of board and care home? Had they skipped out of their Special Ed classes across town? But I sensed if I asked too many questions, they might run out of the bus station and into the Tenderloin where they would soon be exploited.

Choosing not to confront them about their job quest or ages, their faces lit up when I asked if they wanted something to eat. As our volunteer watched the Travelers Aid booth, I took them over to the Greyhound coffee shop. Because the cozy and convenient restaurant was just off the Greyhound lobby, I felt they would be more comfortable there. Maybe they would open up and tell me what was really going on.

As the boys enjoyed their burgers and fries, they told me their names were Lenny and Ronnie, but I couldn't get much else out of them. So I decided to take another approach. Breaking it down as simply as I could, I described my job with Travelers Aid. I explained I was a social worker and that I helped people who were in trouble. Sometimes I helped old people in trouble, sometimes I helped women in trouble—and sometimes I even helped kids in trouble. When I said "kids in trouble," they exchanged glances and shifted nervously in their chairs. Pretending not to notice their discomfort, I took my job description a step further.

"Let's say, for example, that the two of you were in trouble. You're in San Francisco. Somehow you end up in the bus station, but don't know what to do. Would you believe I actually get paid by Travelers Aid to be here in the Greyhound to help people like you?"

Now the boys were really squirming. I concluded the "hypothetical" example by making my calculated appeal: "So, if you *were* in trouble and asked for my assistance, I would do everything I could to help you because that's my job. I would be like your own personal social worker. That means I wouldn't be working for your parents or the police or anyone else. I'd be working for *you*." I paused for a moment, hoping that my words had hit the mark.

Lenny spoke right up. "So if you're our social worker that means you don't tell nobody nothin'—right?" Realizing his question was actually more of a demand, I said I wouldn't talk to anyone without first talking to them. With this, Lenny finally opened up and told me their story.

"Yesterday me and Ronnie ran away from the state hospital. We couldn't take it no more. We hate it there. They always talk about us going to a care home, but nothin' ever happens. We don't want to stay in the hospital. It's a awful place for kids."

Then Ronnie broke in. "Yeah, the food's no good and the other kids aren't like us. They can't hardly talk. We don't have no one to play with." He said his roommate—not Lenny—wet his bed every night and that the room always "smelt like pee." And there was a "fat nurse" he "hated" who picked on them. She was always telling them they would be going to a group home, but it never happened. Lenny said she was "a liar" and that he "hated" the fat nurse too. They wanted to get away from her and the hospital "so bad" they finally ran away. They'd snuck out the night before and hitchhiked to San Francisco. Their last ride dropped them at the Greyhound.

"Our parents don't care," said Lenny. "If they find out where we're at, they'll just send us back to the hospital. They're the ones who sent us there in the first place. We never did nothin' to nobody. Doctors say we're retarded, so we got put in the hospital. We might be kids, but it don't mean we're stupid." When I asked what he meant about being "kids," he reluctantly admitted that he and Ronnie weren't really eighteen. He was fourteen and Ronnie was thirteen. He seemed to be studying me as he spoke, wondering if I would now betray them. I reminded them I wasn't about to call anyone without talking to them first—we'd work together to come up with a good plan. They would just have to trust their new social worker.

I knew California was making a concerted effort to move people out of state hospitals and into the community. The days of warehousing adults and children in hospitals were supposedly over. Barring other overriding factors, individuals with special needs were to be placed in residential care homes in a more normal community setting. This "normalization process" was now the standard approach for dealing with most developmentally disabled people. And while these two boys obviously needed supervision, there seemed no good reason to keep them in a state hospital. Unless I was missing something, a community group home would be a much more appropriate placement.

But their situation was complicated, and we would need some good legal advice on how to proceed. What kind of protection did the law provide children in cases like this? Were there valid reasons for them to be in the state hospital, or were their legal rights being violated? Fortunately, there was a local organization that could help answer these questions. Legal Services for Children offered free legal advice to kids—and it was just two blocks from the Greyhound.

I ran it by the boys. Now that they had their own personal social worker, how would they like to have their own lawyer too? He could become part of our team and help us decide what to do. They were excited and agreed I could make an appointment—which I did. Probably having watched one too many courtroom dramas on TV, Lenny exclaimed, "Tell that fat nurse to talk to our lawyer!" "Yeah," agreed Ronnie, "don't talk to us, talk to our lawyer!" With that they broke into great peals of laughter.

Back at the Travelers Aid booth after their meal, I explained we still had a big problem. Because they were minors—under eighteen—Travelers Aid couldn't get them a room anywhere without their parents' permission. We had an arrangement with the YMCA Hotel to house kids, but we had to have their parents' okay to put them there. The boys weren't happy with this prospect and kept insisting that I not talk with their parents.

"No calls," Lenny insisted. "You promised no calls." I reminded him we would only place calls that were necessary to make our plan work, and getting them a safe place to stay was an important part of our plan. They needed to be somewhere besides the Greyhound—and no, my boss would *not* let them stay at my house.

So I came up with a compromise—I told them that while I had to get their parents' permission for them to stay in a hotel, I didn't have to tell their parents the *name* of the hotel. They liked that idea and agreed I could make the call. With the boys providing their parents' names and the towns where they lived,

I was able to track down the necessary phone numbers from directory assistance. They wanted to listen when I talked with their parents, but were too nervous to stick around. They opted instead to play pinball across the lobby with the quarters I gave them.

My calls to their parents went well. The hospital had already notified them about the boys running away, and they were relieved to hear they were safe and that Travelers Aid was working with them. The two families shared the same basic story. Both boys had behavior problems, but they were not dangerous or criminal. Their parents simply weren't able to handle them at home and felt their other children were being adversely affected.

Because Lenny and Ronnie had both been clinically diagnosed as "mentally retarded," their parents were advised to place them in the state hospital until an appropriate group home was found in the community. They'd been told the hospitalizations would be short-term, but months had gone by and no placements had been made. They were concerned the process was taking so long, but there was no way they could bring the boys back home.

Both families were cooperative and gave me permission to get the boys a hotel room. The parents respected my need for confidentiality—they knew it was important for me to keep the boys' trust and didn't press me for further details. They were just glad their children were safe. I let them know we would be working with the hospital and would keep them updated.

When the boys returned from playing pinball, I told them their parents seemed concerned and had given me permission to get them a room. I assured them I hadn't disclosed the name of the hotel or even the city they were in. They were relieved that I'd respected their confidentiality, but Lenny questioned their parents' sincerity. "If they're so concerned about us," he asked, "how come they sent us to the state hospital?"

After I called the YMCA Hotel and reserved a room for them, we picked up some food before heading over to the hotel. After checking them in—they thought this was all pretty neat—I told them not to leave their room and to keep the door locked. They should stay right there until I returned in the morning. They promised they would.

The next day Lenny and Ronnie were full of stories about all the strange happenings they'd witnessed on the streets below—they stayed up most of the night watching television and looking out their sixth-floor window. When they finally settled down, I told them they had an appointment that afternoon with a lawyer at Legal Services for Children. A Travelers Aid volunteer would get them some fresh clothes, buy them lunch, and then take them over to the lawyer's office. They were disappointed that I couldn't go with them because I had other obligations, but I assured them we would get together at the Greyhound after their appointment.

Later in the afternoon, the volunteer brought the boys to the bus station; everything had gone well and I was to call their lawyer right away. When I phoned the attorney, he said things looked good for Lenny and Ronnie. He'd already talked with the state hospital and both of their parents and, sure enough, the two boys had gotten lost in the system and should have been placed into the community long ago. It turned out they were hospitalized on a voluntary basis—the hospital actually had no grounds to keep them against their will. The lawyer noted that running away had definitely worked in their favor. An embarrassed state hospital was now being legally forced to do what it should have done months ago—find suitable placements for both of the boys.

The attorney said that a hospital social worker was making arrangements for Lenny to be placed in a special group home in Santa Barbara. In fact, he wouldn't even have to return to the hospital. Because he was slightly lower functioning, Ronnie would be placed in another group home that was nearby, which meant they'd be able to visit each other and stay in touch. Ronnie would only have to go back to the state hospital for several days before moving to his new home. The lawyer gave me the name of the hospital social worker so we could coordinate travel arrangements and I thanked him for all his help. Legal Services for Children had been a great resource for Lenny and Ronnie.

When I told the boys the good news, they could hardly believe it. Their days at the state hospital were finally over, and while they were disappointed they wouldn't be in the same group home, they were glad they'd still be able to see each other.

The next day, after all the arrangements had been made, I put the boys on the same Greyhound bus heading south to Santa Barbara. Someone from Lenny's group home would be meeting him and taking him to his new residence. Ronnie would be met separately by a social worker from the state hospital.

The two "blood brothers" had pulled off an amazing coup. With help from Travelers Aid and Legal Services for Children, the state hospital system had been forced to do what it should have done as a matter of course—release them back into the community.

Hugging Lenny and Ronnie good-bye, I realized how attached I had become to these two special boys. They had sensed an injustice in their lives and had done what they could to make things right. I was pleased to have been a part of their happy solution, and I knew they would be a welcome addition to their new homes and communities. As they boarded the Greyhound bus, Ronnie turned around with a big smile on his face and shouted, "Hey Warren, no more fat nurse!" Breaking into their characteristic peals of laughter, he and Lenny waved goodbye as they disappeared into the bus—and were still waving from a window as their bus departed. They were off on a whole new adventure.

Assisting people with special needs was part of what Travelers Aid was all about. With Lenny and Ronnie, it was helping them to get out of the state hospital and back into the community. With a couple from Carbon Glow, Kentucky, it was helping them to do something they had always wanted to do—get married.

The Daltons

For this cause shall a man leave his father and mother,
and shall be joined unto his wife...

—Ephesians 5:31

Y ou would never bump into this particular couple at Macy's or
Banana Republic. Nor would you find them eating at some
fancy restaurant or vacationing in Miami Beach. They were simple
people with simple needs. In their mid-thirties, Norville Dalton
and Esther Jenkins were like two characters out of a *Li'l Abner*
comic strip. They even hailed from the same state, Kentucky, as
Abner and Daisy Mae, but their home was Carbon Glow instead
of Dogpatch. He was unskilled but willing to do any kind of
work; she had a history of hospitalizations for mental problems
and was developmentally disabled. Because of her disabilities, she
was probably eligible for Supplemental Security Income (SSI), but
she had never applied.

Since arriving in the city in their old car, Norville had been
unable to find any kind of work. But even though they were
homeless and out of money, their chief concern was getting
Norville his false teeth—he'd left them at his parents' home in
Carbon Glow before leaving for San Francisco. After talking
with his father on our phone, Norville happily exclaimed, "Sure
as shootin', they was still on the TV table right where I left 'em!"
His father would forward them on to him, care of our office.

While Norville clearly loved Esther and affectionately called
her "the Missus," they had never married. He said they always
wanted to "tie the knot," but it seemed "too dang complicated,"
especially since none of their "kinfolk" thought it was a good

idea and refused to help them get properly "hitched." They came to realize that if they were to have a life together, they would have to leave their families and hometown behind. So they headed out West. Running out of money even before leaving Kentucky, donated gas vouchers and nights in homeless shelters got them to Eugene, Oregon and then to San Francisco.

"How did you get from Eugene to here?" I asked.

After putting some "chewin' tobacco" in his mouth, Norville explained, "Why the folks at some place gave us money for gas and told us to head on down to Frisco and to go to Travelers Aid when we got there—and here we are! But now we got this new idea. We seen this *Grizzly Adams* show on TV and was thinkin' maybe we'd move to the mountains and be with the animals—you know, live off the land."

Norville was serious and Esther was nodding her head in agreement. I told them life in the mountains could be rougher than it appeared on a television show and that they might want to come up with another plan—which they did.

Their alternative strategy was to stay with Esther's cousin Sarah, who lived an hour south of the city in San Jose. When we called, Sarah said the couple could stay with her as long as they liked, and that she'd even wire them some money for gas. After we got off the phone, I urged Esther to apply for SSI in San Jose—maybe Sarah could help her with the paperwork. We then phoned Norville's father and told him to send the false teeth to Sarah's house instead of Travelers Aid. After picking up the wired gas money, Norville and Esther drove off to the cousin's house in San Jose.

A month or so later, Esther and Norville were back in San Francisco. They'd been at her cousin's home for only two weeks before becoming restless. Traveling around the South Bay, they slept in several Salvation Army shelters until Esther's recurring mental health problems resulted in a brief hospitalization in Redwood City. A social worker at the hospital helped her to apply for SSI. When Esther was released from the hospital they returned to San Francisco. Norville said they just wanted to stop by and let me know they were back in the city and staying at the Raphael House shelter for women and families.

It was good to see Norville and Esther again. I really liked them and was touched by their simple devotion to one another. They were an amazingly resilient couple. Even with their handicaps and all that was going on in their lives, Norville and Esther's affection for each other was very apparent. Norville told me they'd met in Carbon Glow and had been together for over ten years. Love can be a hard thing to define, but these two people had it. Their life together was full of problems but it was also full of love. Many couples abandon ship when things get rough, but Norville and Esther had been there for each other through thick and thin.

Impressed by their commitment to one another and convinced that their heart's desire was to be legally married, I was the one who popped the big question: "If I could help you get through all the red tape, how would you two like to get married?"

The answer was an immediate and enthusiastic "Yes!" But who would perform the ceremony, Esther wondered? They were concerned because they didn't belong to a local church. I told them not to worry because there was a church—Glide Memorial Church—just several blocks from our office. With Glide's experience in helping the homeless and the hungry, I was sure that getting the two of them married would be a fairly simple process—and it was.

The next week, after being guided through all the necessary legal hoops, the happy couple was married in the Glide sanctuary by one of the senior ministers. I can attest to the legitimacy of the ceremony because I had the honor of being the best man. With clothes given to them by the church, Norville and Esther were dressed for the occasion when they exchanged their vows. At the right moment, I handed them the rings they'd purchased at a local pawnshop with money donated by their sympathetic social worker. It was a wonderful occasion for everyone present—I even kissed the bride. They were now Norville and Esther Dalton.

Because no couple should stay in a homeless shelter on their wedding night, I gave the newlyweds one of our contracted rooms at the Coronado Hotel and dubbed their room "The Honeymoon Suite" for this special occasion. There were still many hurdles before them, but one thing was certain—for richer or for poorer, for better or for worse, the endearing and enduring couple from Carbon Glow, Kentucky was finally married.

And while the Daltons were hoping to settle down in San Francisco, another Travelers Aid client was about to sail around the world. But first he needed a little help from Travelers Aid.

Captain William Scott

...he doth catch the poor, when he draweth him into his net.

—Psalm 10:9

Sometimes on the weekend I would do my case notes in our office on Mason Street. It was usually much quieter than the bus station—but not always. Writing up some cases one Saturday, I glanced out our second story window and saw a swarm of police cars pull up in front of the Ambassador Hotel across the street. With rifles drawn, the police stormed the old hotel known for its marginal rates and sometimes marginal guests. Almost at once the police emerged with two handcuffed suspects who were placed face down on the sidewalk as still more police cars arrived on the scene.

Watching this high-tension drama unfold, I saw a midget drinking a bottle of wine as he stood on the curb with a man I recognized as a former Travelers Aid client. Moments later, the midget disappeared up Eddy Street walking arm-in-arm with a local hooker in high heels who looked to be twice his size. Meanwhile, several Indian women dressed in brightly colored saris shopped at the open fruit market adjoining the Ambassador. Seemingly oblivious to the police activity next door, they picked through the various fruits and vegetables that were piled high before them. Across the way to my left, people sat in Mike's Athens Greek Restaurant where I often ate Mike's delicious homemade *moussaka*.

As officers put the two handcuffed men in the back of separate police cars, an airport shuttle was heading up Mason Street to drop off passengers at the nearby Hilton Hotel. When the police cars pulled away and the crowd of people in front of the Ambassador slowly dispersed, things went back to "normal." As I returned to my case notes, I thought to myself— just another day in the Tenderloin.

But as I wrote up my cases in the office one Saturday afternoon several months later, there were no policemen storming the Ambassador Hotel and it was all quiet on the Tenderloin front. About the time I was finishing my paperwork, I was paged by the answering service and patched through to a Captain William Scott. He said he'd been robbed after arriving in town from San Diego. Since he wasn't far away, I told him to come directly to our office and I would try to help. A few minutes later a man in his fifties wearing dark slacks, a short-sleeved white shirt, and a captain's hat came to our door. He had an English accent and his face was tanned and weatherworn. I led the seemingly pleasant but distraught captain upstairs where we sat and talked.

"I'm frightfully embarrassed to be here," he said. "I have never been in this kind of a situation." He showed me a copy of his sailing papers and a picture ID that identified him as Captain William Scott. He told me he worked for a wealthy Texas oilman named Herbert Pennington Fraser. His employer owned a small fleet of luxury yachts, and they sailed around the world to various yachting events. The previous week they had been in San Diego with two of their yachts. During their stay, Mr. Fraser purchased two more yachts. He asked Captain Scott to fly to San Francisco to hire two new crews to man the additional yachts. While Captain Scott was hiring the new men, Mr. Fraser and skeleton crews would sail the four yachts up to the Bay Area from San Diego. The boats would remain moored in Oakland for a week or two while they trained the new crew members, then it was on to their next yachting event in Vancouver, British Columbia.

Captain Scott described how he'd flown into San Francisco earlier that morning but had been robbed at gunpoint on Mission Street after arriving at the Greyhound on the airport bus. The thief had taken all of his money and credit cards. After he'd filled out a crime report, the police had put him in touch with the Coast Guard, who used ship-to-shore radio to inform Mr. Fraser of the robbery. Mr. Fraser then relayed that they expected to encounter some offshore storms near Santa Barbara and wouldn't be arriving in the Bay Area until the middle of the week. He suggested that in the meantime Captain Scott should contact Travelers Aid for assistance. Mr. Fraser mentioned he was a longtime patron of Travelers Aid. He described it as a "worthy and helpful organization" that would probably assist Captain Scott until they arrived in Oakland. Mr. Fraser said he would reimburse Travelers Aid for any expense incurred on the Captain's behalf.

I told Captain Scott that robberies were common in the inner city. I recounted how one of my co-workers had been robbed at knifepoint near the Greyhound one evening and how I had surprised a burglar late one night who'd broken into our Travelers Aid office from the second story window of the adjacent Bristol Hotel. Fortunately for me, the burglar fled back out our window when he heard me coming. I then went on to tell the marooned Captain that we would house him at the nearby Coronado Hotel and provide him with food vouchers until their yachts arrived, and that I would be back in the office on Tuesday if he needed anything further.

Captain Scott seemed relieved and grateful that he could now attend to the business of hiring the new crew members. He said they preferred to hire in San Francisco and through organizations like Salvation Army and Goodwill rather than the Sailor's Union; it was more economical, and the men they hired through these groups were usually less demanding and more appreciative of the work. The jobs didn't require a seafaring background; any motivated, hard-working individual could learn the necessary tasks and procedures. He asked if I knew anyone who might be interested in hiring on for a year—the pay was good and a gourmet chef prepared all their meals.

Intrigued by the notion of sailing around the world, and only half-jokingly, I asked if he would consider hiring someone like me. Much to my surprise he said he'd hire me right on the spot; for a fleeting moment I imagined myself sailing to exotic ports, far away from the troubles of the inner city. But those thoughts quickly passed, and I told him that while his offer was tempting, I really liked my job with Travelers Aid. Noting my obvious interest and smiling, he said he'd check back with me the next time they sailed into San Francisco.

Addressing his need to hire workers, I gave Captain Scott a map of the area and directions to the offices of Salvation Army and Goodwill. He said he would go to both of them on Monday morning. I also gave him directions to the Coronado Hotel.

As we continued talking, Captain Scott showed me a photo of his house in the Bahamas, but added he was rarely there. He confessed he was most at home on the sea. Sailing had been his passion and his life for as long as he could remember.

When we finished talking, I gave Captain Scott his vouchers and one of my business cards. He said it was easy to understand why his employer was a longtime contributor to Travelers Aid, and reiterated that we would be reimbursed when Mr. Fraser and the yachts arrived.

Before leaving, he extended a special invitation for me and my girlfriend to join him for a formal dinner on Mr. Fraser's personal yacht the following Saturday night. He wrote down the slip number at the Oakland Marina where the yachts would be moored. Dinner would be served at "1800 hours sharp." He told me to wear a coat and tie and that my girlfriend should wear a dress. Flattered by the offer, I accepted his invitation. As I drove home after work, I was already looking forward to dinner aboard Mr. Fraser's yacht that coming Saturday night.

Returning to the office on Tuesday afternoon, there was an urgent message for me to call the Director of Goodwill Industries. When I reached him he asked if I knew a Captain William Scott. I said I did, and had referred the Captain to Goodwill and Salvation Army to possibly hire some men for an extended yachting expedition. The director told me that Captain Scott arrived at their Goodwill store the previous morning and had presented my Travelers Aid card to him as a reference: He needed to hire ten men to work on two new yachts his employer had purchased in San Diego. The new hires would be sailing around the world to various yachting events. Seeing it as a great opportunity, the director arranged for the Captain to make a formal presentation after lunch in their Goodwill office.

Captain Scott addressed the Goodwill staff and the hopeful group of unemployed men the director had hastily assembled for the occasion. The Captain explained that the new crew members would receive good pay and great food as they sailed around the world the next year. In fact, it was such a compelling presentation the director thought he was going to lose half his staff. After the talk, Captain Scott interviewed potential crew members and hired ten men right then and there. Because the yachts would be leaving Oakland in less than two weeks, the Captain said he needed to purchase their uniforms immediately. After taking the men's measurements, he asked each man to make a fifty-dollar "good faith" deposit on the uniforms—this would help cover the costs should anyone change their mind about the job after the uniforms were altered. The money would be refunded in their first paycheck.

This was quite a sacrifice for most of the men: For many it took every cent they had, while others borrowed money from friends and family. But by late Monday afternoon they had paid Captain Scott the necessary deposits. The Captain proceeded to invite the newly hired men—and the entire Goodwill staff—to the Hilton Hotel for breakfast the next morning at "0900" to celebrate the hiring of the new crew.

They all went to the Hilton Hotel at the prescribed time to meet Captain Scott for the celebratory breakfast—but Captain Scott never showed up. Worse yet, the AWOL Captain still had the $500 the ten men had scraped together for their uniforms. The director asked if I had any idea where the "good" Captain might be found. Stunned by his account and feeling awful about what happened, I told him I was sorry to say that I had no idea where Captain Scott might be. However, as I thought about it, I knew one place where the Captain would *not* be found—eating dinner on Saturday night with me and my girlfriend at the Oakland Marina.

I was usually pretty good at screening people's stories, but an urban pirate calling himself Captain William Scott had shanghaied everyone. He took us for a ride, but it wasn't on one of Mr. Fraser's fancy yachts. I don't know if it was his English accent, his sailing papers, his purported house in the Bahamas, or the story about his wealthy employer, but it never occurred to me that "Captain Scott" was just another Tenderloin-type con man.

While Captain Scott apparently traveled from town to town deceiving people, Walt traveled from town to town selling tickets to the circus.

The Telephone Salesman

*Sorrow is better than laughter: for by the sadness
of the countenance the heart is made better.*

—Ecclesiastes 7:3

I was in the main office early one evening doing some paperwork when my beeper sounded and the answering service patched me through to a man with a smooth baritone voice named Walt. Because he was near the office, I told him to come right over.

Dressed in a suit and tie, Walt was a tall, portly, middle-aged man with a thick black mustache. While presenting a friendly, confident demeanor, he was sweating heavily and was obviously under a lot of pressure. He'd just arrived in the city to sell tickets for the circus that was in town, but had gotten drunk the night before and blown all the money he'd set aside for food and housing—and he wouldn't be paid again until the end of the week. He'd done the same thing in New Orleans once and had received help from their local Travelers Aid. He knew we weren't in the business of assisting people who drank away their paychecks, but he didn't know where else to turn. Walt knew he had a drinking problem, but said he was usually responsible with his money.

I told him I appreciated his honesty and agreed to house him for three nights at the Coronado Hotel until he received his paycheck at the end of the week. When I gave him the necessary vouchers, he was very relieved and thanked me heartily. But as he started to leave, I realized he needed to talk more. When I invited him to stay a while longer, he was glad to sit down again.

Walt proceeded to tell me about the circus and his job as a traveling ticket salesman. His life on the road was lonely, but selling circus tickets seemed the best way for him to make a living—he was good on the phone and had been doing it for years. I told him about my telephone sales job with Time-Life Books when I first came to San Francisco. We agreed that some of the people we contacted were very nice and some were very rude—and that hang-ups were no fun.

He was intrigued I'd done similar work. Walt was interested in the fact that our Time-Life offices were in the same Market Street building where *The Maltese Falcon* author Dashiell Hammett was once employed as a Pinkerton detective—and that I had sold a set of Time-Life photography books to blues singer John Lee Hooker. As we swapped telephone stories back and forth, he knew that I understood the ups and downs of trying to connect with strangers on the telephone.

Then, out of the blue, Walt asked my birth date. When I told him October 21st, he said that *had* to be the reason he felt so comfortable with me. *He* was a Libra also. The fact that we shared the same astrological sign was obviously important to him and seemed to strengthen the bond he was feeling from our conversation. Trusting me even more, he really opened up. But as he did, his ever-present smile slowly faded away as he became more reflective. He said things had been hard since his wife left him six years ago. Life felt empty and meaningless—a revolving-door cycle of traveling city to city selling circus tickets and getting drunk. There were times when he felt like ending it all. That was when he *really* got drunk—like the night before.

Suddenly aware of how much he was sharing, he instantly shut down the flood of emotion he had been expressing. Pulling himself together, he reassumed the self-assured salesman persona he presented to the world. Then, smiling broadly, he rose to his feet and apologized for talking so much. "Hey, you're a busy man. I didn't mean to take so much of your time. I'd better get going."

It was a remarkable transformation. Everything he had been feeling a few moments before had been neatly compartmentalized and stuffed back inside himself. But as he said good-bye, he let down his guard again—if only for a moment. And as he did, I felt the warmth and sincerity of his parting words.

"I don't usually talk to people this way. My time with you has meant a great deal to me. Thank you—not just for helping me out, but for hearing me out." Acknowledging his words, I encouraged him to hang in there and to try and get some help for his drinking.

Later that night, when I returned to the office from the Greyhound, I found a brown paper bag with my name on it leaning against our office door. I took the bag upstairs and opened it. Inside was a handsome wooden Libra plaque that listed all the assumed virtues of people born under that particular sign. An accompanying note said: "I've carried this with me for the last six years. It has always given me strength and comfort when I needed it most. I want you to have it now. Thanks for everything, Walt." Although I wasn't into astrology, I appreciated the fact that Walt had just given me one of his most prized possessions.

People like Walt were a joy to work with. They helped to offset the occasional unpleasantness of people like the man in my next story. Whereas Walt sold tickets *to* the circus, this man looked like the strong man *in* a circus.

The Strong Man

...behold their threatenings...

—Acts 4:29

In front of our Travelers Aid booth, people walked up and down the stairs to the second floor restrooms. Bathed in the bright glow of the overhead fluorescent lights, passengers were sitting, reading, eating, sleeping, and generally killing time as they waited for their buses to arrive. Strewn about the floor were the usual suitcases, backpacks, briefcases, and baby carriages. The final call for one of the evening buses was being announced: "All aboard please and thanks for going Greyhound—the energy saver."

Speaking of energy, if it wasn't a full-moon night, it might as well have been. Full-moon nights brought some very strange people into the Greyhound. This particular night a short, stocky man with a shaved head, who appeared to be about thirty years old, approached the Travelers Aid booth. He had a wild determined look in his eyes and he reminded me of the strong man in a circus. Glancing around suspiciously and speaking in a low, deliberate manner, he said he wanted to report a murder in Colorado. Glaring at me in a most menacing manner, he said he was an eyewitness and wanted to talk about it.

When I told him it would be best to call the police, he said he didn't want to talk to the police—he wanted to talk to *me*. Then looking deep into my eyes and smiling a twisted kind of crazy smile, he said when I left the Greyhound that night he would be waiting outside to kill me. After that he would chop me into a hundred pieces, pile me in the trunk of his car, and dump me in the desert. With that said, he picked up our Travelers Aid telephone and started talking like Donald Duck. He was laughing hysterically as the Greyhound security guard led him out to the street.

The Tenderloin was filled with disturbed people like the "Strong Man." Many of them had been released from state mental hospitals and migrated to the inner city. It was common to see them talking to themselves on street corners or yelling at passersby. Many were receiving Supplemental Security Income (SSI) because of their mental condition. Some lived in cheap hotels, board-and-care homes, or simply slept on the street. Socially isolated, they wandered aimlessly around the Tenderloin. Most of them were harmless, but some were a danger to themselves and the community.

Was the "Strong Man" serious about killing me? Probably not—but you never know. The wild look in his eyes certainly put me on full alert. Later that night after closing, I didn't exit through the front door as usual. Instead, I slipped out one of the back gates where the buses arrived and departed. I then hurried toward the lot where my car was parked several blocks away.

You have to take precautions with someone like the "Strong Man." In recent years the city had been besieged by a wave of violence that caused even the bravest of citizens to be especially wary. The notorious "Zebra" killers had terrorized San Francisco with their random murders around the city. For no apparent reason, fifteen people had been shot and killed as they walked in local neighborhoods. Two of the shootings were within six blocks of the Greyhound bus station. And while the "Zebra" killers had finally been caught and convicted, the "Zodiac" killer was still on the loose. After haunting the Bay Area for several years, he seemed to disappear. But a new threatening letter was about to surface, warning that he was back.

With all the recent violence in the city, it was a bit unnerving to encounter someone like the "Strong Man." However, when I reached my car he was nowhere in sight. Apparently, he had faded back into the Tenderloin, saving his madness for someone else, some other night. Hopefully I wouldn't be seeing him again.

Walking to my car late at night I always had to be careful. But there was only one other time I felt threatened. Stepping out of the shadows, an aggressive panhandler came at me quite unexpectedly.

The Late-Night Panhandler

If it be possible, as much as lieth in you,
live peaceably with all men.

—Romans 12:18

"Any spare change?" was like a Market Street mantra. Panhandlers were everywhere and they came in all shapes and sizes. Some were legitimately down on their luck. Others were just looking for an easy handout. A short, bald man in his mid-seventies was a familiar sight on Market Street. Dressed in a suit and tie and perfectly shined black shoes, he requested "only a dime" to help him purchase a train ticket to suburban Palo Alto. Many people gave him a dollar—he was so polite and unassuming it was hard for anyone to turn him down. But not all of the downtown panhandlers were so courteous.

One night around ten o'clock I walked back to my car after leaving the Greyhound. I was parked in my usual lot on Mission Street, not far from skid row. As I neared my vehicle, a large burly man stepped out of the shadows. With a deep booming voice he bellowed, "Give me a QUARTER!" As he made his demand, he lumbered toward me on a set of crutches. I could see that his right foot was in a cast and he wore a hospital bracelet on his left wrist. Because of his limited mobility, I was able to elude him by quickly retreating from the parking lot. However, as I ran across Mission Street toward the presumed safety of a corner market, I could see that the aggressive panhandler was following close behind. Galloping, hobbling, and hopping his way toward me, he continued to shout his insistent demand—"Give me a QUARTER!"

Assuming he would leave after I entered the market, I was shocked when he planted himself by the front door and continued to bellow his belligerent request. Standing safely within the store, I was not about to give in to his bullying tactics. Everything I'd learned in life told me not to reward this kind of behavior. I would simply wait him out.

Meanwhile, the employees in the market seemed completely oblivious to what was taking place—how I was essentially being held hostage in their store by this persistent panhandler. While they went nonchalantly about their business, the panhandler kept yelling for me to give him that "QUARTER!" It had been a long day and I wanted to get home—but there was a principle involved and I was determined *not* to give in.

As the minutes ticked by, I kept assuming the man would eventually give up and go away. But that was not happening. From what I could gather, the relentless panhandler was settling in for the long haul. A little while later, perhaps sensing that my determination was wavering, he leaned through the doorway and in a surprisingly normal tone of voice said, "If you give me a quarter, I'll go away."

Carefully considering my alternatives—calling the police, spending the night in the store, or giving in—I walked toward the door and addressed the panhandler. "If I give you a quarter, will you *really* go away?" In that same normal voice, he said he would. So I gave him a quarter and he went away—just like that.

After he departed up Fifth Street, I walked back to my car. As I drove away, I knew the panhandler had trumped me with his clever tactics. But I didn't care. I was out of the store, away from him, and on my way home. Sometimes practicality has to win out over principle.

When it came right down to it, winning my point with the panhandler was not a life-or-death matter. But for a young San Francisco Giants baseball fan, winning *was* a life-or-death matter.

The Giants Fan

Hope deferred maketh the heart sick...
—Proverbs 13:12

Jay was twenty-four years old. He had short dark hair, black-rimmed glasses, and several days growth from not shaving. Slightly overweight and with open sores on both of his pale, white arms, he was carrying a small suitcase, a collapsible fishing rod, and a transistor radio. He was also wearing a San Francisco Giants baseball cap.

Jay told me he had been staying with his uncle in Santa Rosa since being released from Napa State Hospital the previous month. He came to the city looking for work, but things were bad; jobs that had once been so easy to find were gone. In the past he'd been paid to keep score for the neighborhood bowlers on Jones Street, but the lanes had been recently torn down to make room for a new development. His plan was to go to Everton's the next several mornings to get day-work throwing handbills on people's front porches; hopefully he could earn enough money to rent a weekly room at one of the cheap hotels over on Sixth Street. He wouldn't stay in the missions because there were so many people—it reminded him of the state hospital. He asked if we could provide a room for two or three days until he made enough money to pay for his own room. If we couldn't help, he would sleep outside. There were always the tunnels on Folsom Street.

He was relieved when I told him he could stay in one of our rooms at the Coronado Hotel for the next three nights. We would also give him some food vouchers. Hopefully by the end of his stay he would earn enough money to rent a room on Sixth Street. Just in case he had trouble getting work at Everton's, I wrote down the addresses of several other day-labor offices in the area. I also suggested he go to the Department of Social Services to apply for General Assistance.

Knowing he was covered for the next three days, he began to share some of his deeper feelings. He said it was frustrating looking for jobs that weren't there anymore. He didn't need much money and was willing to do anything. He had always been able to get by, but things were different now. It was getting hard to make ends meet. Changing his train of thought, he started talking about the San Francisco Giants baseball team. He said he always listened to their games on his transistor radio and then gave me a complete rundown of all their starting players. As he went from position to position, he grew more and more animated. But his demeanor completely changed when he began describing the "awful" season the Giants were having—their play was terrible and they were way down in the league standings. Becoming very emotional and struggling for words, he then told me what was *really* on his mind. "Two days ago I almost killed myself."

He described how he had been following the Giants baseball team for years. However, since his release from the hospital, they'd been playing their worst baseball ever. He said there was no reason for them to be that bad. They had a good pitching staff and strong hitters, but they continued to lose game after game—and as they kept losing, he found himself getting more and more depressed. Two days before, with the Giants losing yet another game, he said he couldn't take it anymore. Standing high above the Pacific Ocean near Land's End, with the game on the radio and the Giants facing certain defeat, he was ready to jump. The game, the season, his life—everything seemed so hopeless and disappointing. But then late in the game the Giants started to rally. In an incredible turn of events, they came from behind to win the game with a last-inning home run. Jay said he was so relieved, he lost his desire to jump. Maybe the Giants would get better and maybe his life would get better too.

As I listened to Jay, my heart went out to this young man with the transistor radio, collapsible fishing rod, and Giants baseball cap. All alone in the city, he was willing to do any kind of work in order to survive. He faced many challenges, but who would have guessed that the meaning of his life was so intertwined with the fortunes of a major-league baseball team? After expressing my concern about his suicidal feelings, I convinced him to go to the Tenderloin Clinic. He was familiar with the clinic because he had seen a counselor there before going to the state hospital.

I called the clinic and made an emergency referral. An intake worker talked with Jay on the phone and told him to come right over. Because Travelers Aid was short-term and crisis-oriented, we had to rely on agencies like the Tenderloin Clinic to provide the long-term counseling and case management required for people like Jay. They would give him some of the support he so desperately needed and help him follow through with the Department of Social Services and maybe apply for SSI.

Jay left for the clinic after I gave him the vouchers for his food and lodging. When I called over there later, I was glad to hear he made his appointment and that his former counselor would be seeing him on a regular basis.

I never saw Jay again after that day, but I often wondered what happened to him. I wanted to believe that he'd found a job and some kind of happiness. Hopefully his emotional well-being was no longer dependent on the success or failure of his favorite baseball team. But I have to admit that, even to this day, I find myself thinking of Jay whenever I hear that the San Francisco Giants have been on a particularly long losing streak.

Jay gave literal meaning to the term "die-hard" baseball fan. Waldo Weinstein was also a fan of the game. But while Jay *internalized* his baseball disappointments by taking out his frustrations on himself, Waldo *externalized* his frustrations by screaming at the umpires and just about everyone else.

Waldo Weinstein

Rejoice with them that do rejoice, and weep with them that weep.

—Romans 12:15

Late one Saturday afternoon, Waldo Weinstein showed up at the Greyhound. Although he wasn't a Travelers Aid client, he had been on my caseload when I worked as an eligibility worker for the San Francisco Department of Social Services several years earlier. Because of our past relationship, he would often check in with me at the Greyhound.

Waldo was a short, loveable, red-haired, freckle-faced fireball. He was both developmentally disabled and emotionally disturbed. But in his own inimitable way, he was sharp as a tack and funny as can be. He was receiving a monthly SSI check and living with his old-fashioned, no-nonsense Jewish parents. Although he was nearly thirty, he looked and acted like a hyper-kinetic teenager. Waldo was always on the go.

Because of his short legs and squat stature, he walked with a shuffle—taking small rapid steps as he hurried from place to place. He wore large, tortoise-shell glasses that framed his twinkling yet ever-mischievous brown eyes. His disproportionately large head was covered with thick, curly, red hair. He spoke with a pronounced New York accent and always seemed to have a sardonic smile on his face. With his characteristic smirk, he was very adept at rolling off hilarious one-liners about a world that didn't know what to do with him. Waldo knew that most people regarded him as a freak—and it broke his heart.

He was often accompanied by his equally short and overprotective mother. When he came to the bus station alone, he was usually in some kind of trouble. This particular day he was by himself and more agitated than ever. He said he was running away from home and was on his way to New York City. Although Waldo had been running away more frequently, he rarely left the Bay Area and was usually back home in a day or two. But this afternoon he was really upset.

"Warren, I've had it with my parents! Every week on TV it's Donny and Marie! Donny and Marie! I want outta here! I'm going to New York City! Gimme a ticket!"

He was very insistent as he tried to manipulate me in his forceful yet endearing manner. Hoping to justify his need for a ticket, he told me the Red Sox would be playing at Yankee Stadium. Waldo loved baseball.

He knew I couldn't give him a ticket, but it was his way of letting me know how bad things were. At times like this, we would talk awhile and then he would usually go home. But this afternoon he screamed at me for not giving him a ticket. He said no one understood him and he was sick of it. Before I knew it, he ran out of the bus station and disappeared up Seventh Street. I was especially concerned because I'd never seen him quite like that.

Several weeks later, Waldo's mother stopped by the Greyhound to tell me that Waldo had been picked up jaywalking in Los Angeles. He'd been ranting and raving about the owner of the Oakland Athletics baseball team. Waldo had a way of projecting his anger onto various celebrities, and I was very aware of the interplay between Waldo's childlike enthusiasm and his deep-seated hurt and anger. They were integral parts of his unique personality.

Two years before, I'd taken him to Candlestick Park to watch a San Francisco Giants baseball game. With his ever-present smirk, biting humor, and taunting comments to the umpires, he had everyone around us laughing hysterically. But when I took him for a walk around Lake Merced, he caught me completely off guard with his heartfelt sincerity—"Warren, I like Lake Merced." His inquisitive nature and simple appreciation for things was incredibly genuine. When I drove him down to Half Moon Bay, he wanted to know everything he could about this seaside area that immediately became his favorite town. "Warren, does Half Moon Bay have a newspaper? Warren, does Half Moon Bay have apartments to rent? Warren, do you think I could ever live in Half Moon Bay?"

The world was an endlessly fascinating yet frustrating place for Waldo. I doubted things would change much until he had more independence—perhaps living in a supportive group home away from his well-intentioned but controlling parents. Until then, he would probably continue to be in and out of hospitals and mental health clinics.

Waldo's dreams were modest by everyday standards. For instance, he desperately wanted to drive a car. It was almost an obsession with him. He felt if he could get his psychiatrist's permission to take the state driving exam, then he could get his driver's license and be like everyone else. But his doctor—for very good reasons—wouldn't sign a release.

"Warren, I hate my stupid shrink!" he would tell me with his inimitable disdain. He also talked of having his own apartment—"So I can play rock music and not have to watch Donny and Marie." But perhaps more than anything he wanted a girlfriend—"One like yours, Warren, only Jewish and in my size." These dreams of having a driver's license, an apartment, and a girlfriend were ones that most men easily attain. Waldo would be fortunate to get even one of them.

I recalled the night several years earlier when my former girlfriend Anne and I invited Waldo over for dinner. We were having a good time talking about everything. Waldo always enjoyed hearing stories about my Army days working for the White House—how I met President Johnson and his wife Lady Bird, and sometimes served as a courier to Air Force One. He especially loved hearing how I accompanied the Vice-President to the 1969 All Star baseball game played at Robert F. Kennedy Stadium—and that another White House worker and I had spent the whole game in the National League dugout with our childhood heroes. Waldo would have given anything to be in that dugout with us.

After the meal and much laughter, Waldo was as relaxed as I had ever seen him. But at some point the continual jokes and nervous chatter ceased and he became unusually serious. With tremendous anguish, he described several of the mental hospitals where he'd been sent. In great detail he recounted being teased and beaten by the boys in his unit. He mourned the fact that he didn't fit in anywhere—"Warren, do you think I'll *ever* be happy?"

At some point in the conversation, Anne had left the table and was in the kitchen wiping her eyes with a Kleenex. She felt for him as he was in so much emotional pain. But after another ten minutes or so of heart-wrenching catharsis, Waldo suddenly shifted gears. Instantly, he was back to his exuberant hyper-kinetic self—describing all the cities he had been to that had major-league baseball parks and telling us what he thought of their teams.

I saw Waldo many times after that night, but he never again spoke of his time in state mental hospitals. It was easier for him to heap ridicule and contempt on the world than to talk about the ridicule and contempt the world had heaped on him. There were many people who came and went down at the bus station, but there was never anyone quite like Waldo Weinstein.

Michael was another young man with a great deal of inner anguish. When I met him at the Greyhound, he told me why he was in such distress.

The Accident

Blessed are they that mourn: for they shall be comforted.

—Matthew 5:4

The Travelers Aid booth often served as a way station for people passing through San Francisco. They weren't our clients per se, but were figuratively "out of gas" and needing encouragement. Sometimes we were like a Greyhound confessional—a safe, anonymous place where weary travelers could unload the emotional burdens they were carrying around. That was the case with Michael. He wasn't asking for anything. He was just trying to find the best way to hitchhike out of the city.

In his early twenties, Michael looked like someone who had gone to prep school or an Ivy League college. He was wearing brown corduroy pants, a yellow Shetland sweater, and penny loafers. His brown hair was neatly combed and he was carrying a small backpack. He was someone's handsome son, but he was a long way from his Pennsylvania hometown.

When I asked him what he was up to, he told me he'd been hitchhiking around the country, traveling from place to place ever since…"the accident." With the word "accident" hanging in the air, I asked if he wanted to talk about what happened. After some initial hesitation he said that, yes, it probably was time he talked about it with someone. He then told me about the accident.

A year ago, he and his cousin Rusty were returning home from a long trip when Michael fell asleep at the wheel and the car crashed. He survived; Rusty did not. He knew there was nothing he could do to change things, but he couldn't get the accident out of his mind. Haunted by his cousin's death and unable to forgive himself for what happened, he'd hit the road. Staying in motion was the only way he could cope. Nearly in tears, he said he felt terrible and wished he had died rather than Rusty.

I told Michael that somehow he had to forgive himself for what happened and that Rusty would not want him to be living the way he was. I suggested that he stop long enough somewhere to get support. If he wanted, we could help him settle in San Francisco and get some counseling. He thought about it for a moment, but said he wasn't ready to do that yet. Continuing to share extensively on a deep emotional level, he said it was good talking with someone and thanked me for listening—things had gotten pretty bottled up inside and just talking about it made him feel a little better. I told him that if the sincerity and magnitude of one's sorrow could earn forgiveness, he had surely earned that forgiveness a hundred times over.

When I asked Michael where he was off to, he smiled and said wherever his next ride took him. As we said good-bye I told him that for whatever it was worth, I forgave him for what happened—and hoped that someday he would forgive himself. Back then God's forgiveness was an unfamiliar concept to me, but in retrospect it was probably what Michael needed most. Hopefully, in time, he found that forgiveness and was delivered from his self-imposed penance of endlessly traveling from town to town.

Sometimes the road can feel like your only friend as people try to make sense of their lives. José was another one of these inveterate travelers.

Homeless at the Hyatt

They wandered the wilderness in a solitary way;
they found no city to dwell in.

—Psalm 107:4

José, a shy, soft-spoken Hispanic man in his early twenties, came to the Travelers Aid booth one Friday night requesting food and lodging. He told me he was homeless, yet on our application he listed the Hyatt Regency as his current address. When I asked him about it, he said he had been sleeping in the janitor's closet, but the cramped quarters and smell of cleaning solvents made sleeping very difficult.

José was hitching out of the city the next day and hoped Travelers Aid would give him a room so he could get a good night's sleep. When I inquired about possible resources, he said his family was on the East Coast but would have nothing to do with him because he was gay.

Since it was almost time to close our booth for the night, I went ahead and gave him our open room at the Coronado. It was stretching our policies a bit as we generally referred people with transient lifestyles to the rescue missions, but he looked so tired and run-down I made a late night exception. I felt it would not only provide him with some desperately needed rest, but would also let him know that someone cared about him.

The next morning José stopped by the Greyhound. He looked refreshed and came by to thank Travelers Aid and say good-bye. With that he was off to another city, another janitor's closet, another sympathetic social worker, or whatever else he could find to keep himself covered.

While José was about to *hitchhike* out of the city, a young businessman was about to *fly* out of the city. But first he needed bus fare to get to the airport.

The Fleeced Businessman

Can a man take fire in his bosom, and his clothes not be burned?
—Proverbs 6:27

A man in a suit and tie—probably in his early thirties— approached the Travelers Aid booth. He had been staying at the Holiday Inn while doing business in the city. With obvious embarrassment, he said he had been "fleeced" the night before "doing things I shouldn't have been doing." The woman whose services he had employed stole his wallet—all he had left was his plane ticket home. His hotel room was paid up, but he had no money for the bus to the airport. He said it would have been too awkward to ask his business associates for money. Could Travelers Aid help him get a bus ticket so he could make his flight? He promised to pay us back right away. His wife would be meeting him at the airport, so he was okay once he arrived in New York.

Greatly relieved after we got him the ticket through Greyhound, he thanked us and hurried off to board his bus. Hopefully he would not be putting himself in that kind of situation again. A week later he returned the fare, along with a contribution to Travelers Aid.

While the young businessman couldn't wait to leave the city, a young woman with a big dream couldn't wait to arrive in the city.

"Amazing Grace"

...one thing I know, that, whereas I was blind, now I see.
—John 9:25

One of Travelers Aid's many responsibilities was to meet young children or vulnerable adults who were traveling alone and help them make their necessary connections. Volunteers usually filled this role, but since a volunteer was unavailable on this particular day, I was asked to assist a legally blind, twenty-five-year-old African-American woman arriving from Los Angeles on a Greyhound bus. She was to have eye surgery at Mt. Zion Medical Center. I was to meet her bus, help with her luggage, and escort her to a waiting cab in front of the bus station.

According to plan, I met the woman's bus at the designated arrival gate. As I secured her luggage and walked her through the lobby, her peaceful demeanor and calm determination impressed me. She was confident the procedure she was about to undergo would restore her sight. And while grateful for my help, she said it wasn't necessary to accompany her to the housing that had been arranged for her near the medical center. She would be met by someone at the facility when her cab arrived. Settling into the taxi, she gave the driver the address of her prearranged housing and they drove off.

Several weeks later, Barbara, our Volunteer Coordinator, informed me that the woman's surgery had been a complete success. The formerly blind young woman now had sight. I don't recall her name, but I will always remember the grace she exuded walking through the Greyhound before her surgery. For this reason she will always be "Amazing Grace" to me—she once was blind, but now could see.

There was another instance when I filled the volunteer role of assisting a vulnerable Greyhound passenger. This time it was a seven-year-old girl from northern California.

Dove

*Whosoever therefore shall humble himself as this little child,
the same is greatest in the kingdom of heaven.*

—Matthew 18:4

Our volunteer hadn't arrived yet, so I was the one approached by the Greyhound ticket agent. A concerned mother living in the coastal town of Mendocino had just contacted him. This quaint village, known for its artists and alternative lifestyles, was located 150 miles north of San Francisco. The woman had called to alert Greyhound that her young daughter, Dove, was traveling by herself on the morning bus from Mendocino to San Francisco. The girl's father was supposed to meet her bus, but had just called to say he was running late. When the mother was informed that the Mendocino bus had already arrived, she became very worried. She knew her daughter was probably sitting somewhere in the bus station feeling frightened and alone.

The mother gave the Greyhound agent a detailed description of her daughter and requested that someone find Dove to let her know that her father would be there soon. The agent asked me to locate the girl and remain with her until the father arrived.

It didn't take me long to find her—she was the little girl with the blonde ponytail sitting by herself in the corner of the lobby. All dressed up to see her dad, she was wearing the matching yellow skirt, yellow blouse, and yellow sneakers that her mother had described. Crying softly, she was bravely trying to read the oversized book that helped to hide her tear-streaked face. The bus station can be very scary when you are only seven years old and your father isn't there to meet your bus.

I walked up to Dove and told her I was with Travelers Aid. I explained how her mother had just called to say that her Dad would be there soon. She was happy to have me stay there with her until her father arrived about ten minutes later.

Claudine was also tearful and afraid, but she was not at the bus station. She was standing at the corner of Jones and Ellis when a stranger persuaded her to call Travelers Aid.

Claudine

They that sow in tears shall reap in joy.

—Psalm 126:5

Claudine was eighteen years old and had traveled down from Seattle three weeks earlier looking for work. Unable to find a job, she quickly ran out of money. Meanwhile, a seemingly pleasant young man invited her to stay in his Tenderloin apartment until she got back on her feet. But a week or so later, he told her she had to start paying him back by "working" the streets. He forced her to stand on the corner of Jones and Ellis and make herself "available." A woman found her on the street crying, and after hearing Claudine's story helped her to call Travelers Aid. She then escorted Claudine over to the bus station.

When I talked with Claudine, she said she was afraid of the man she'd been staying with and what he might do if he found her. All of her belongings were at his apartment, but she wasn't about to return. It would be too dangerous.

She became anxious when I suggested she call her mother in Seattle—they hadn't been on the best of terms when she left. But using our phone, she went ahead and made the call. When her mom said her old bedroom was ready and waiting for her, Claudine broke down and cried. Her mother would even drive to the Seattle Greyhound terminal to prepay her bus ticket home.

She remained with me at the Travelers Aid booth until her ticket was wired and her bus was ready to depart. At the scheduled time I walked Claudine to her bus and watched her board. She was glad to be safe and heading home.

Tenderloin hustlers were extremely clever in the way they moved in on vulnerable young women like Claudine. Patty was also taken in, but on a much deeper level.

The Girl Next Door

Neither give place to the devil.

—Ephesians 4:27

Patty was nineteen. With her long red hair, myriad freckles, radiant blue eyes, and strong New England accent, she had the innocent look of the "girl next door." She was accompanied by her boyfriend—a quiet young man named Tim who had hitchhiked with her from New Hampshire to San Francisco. Having exhausted their funds en route, they'd spent the previous night sleeping behind some rhododendron bushes in Golden Gate Park. Someone in the park told them about Travelers Aid.

Patty and Tim were looking for work and wanted to remain in the city. They seemed motivated and sincere, so I went ahead and housed them at the Coronado for three nights. I also gave them food vouchers, and told them that the Haight-Ashbury Switchboard might help them when they left the Coronado. The switchboard had evolved during the 1967 Summer of Love—the "flower power" era when a flood of hippies and young people determined to "make love, not war" poured into the Haight-Ashbury district that bordered Golden Gate Park. The switchboard's specialty was finding "crash pads" for young people living on the fringe. I also referred them to several agencies that helped people find work.

After three nights at the Coronado, Patty and Tim moved on. Several months later, Patty returned alone. She told me that she and Tim had been "crashing" in people's homes, thanks to the Haight-Ashbury Switchboard. When they finally ran out of places to sleep, Tim went back to New Hampshire—but Patty decided to remain in the city. She worked a temporary job near Hunters Point, but it had ended and she was out of money again with nowhere to stay. She asked if Travelers Aid could possibly put her back at the Coronado Hotel while she resumed looking for employment. She was also applying for General Assistance at the Department of Social Services in case she couldn't find a job. Stretching our guidelines a bit, I housed her again at the Coronado but I stressed the importance of her following through with DSS.

When Patty returned several weeks later, she wasn't asking for anything—she was just "checking in." Appearing upbeat, she described meeting a young man at DSS while applying for assistance. Learning she was homeless, he invited her to stay in his Tenderloin apartment. Patty said he was "really nice" and made her feel "special." She was already calling him her "boyfriend."

In the coming weeks Patty would occasionally stop by the main office before I went down to the bus station. She was still living with her boyfriend, but was beginning to look pale and haggard. One day she confided that her boyfriend was dealing drugs and they were having problems. She loved him, but wanted him to get away from the drugs and the Tenderloin.

The next time I saw Patty, she looked terrible. She had a black eye and her face was red from crying. Her boyfriend had hit her, and now *she* was on drugs. I urged her to leave before things got worse—I could refer her to the women's shelter or even help her return home to New Hampshire. She thanked me for my concern, but said she wanted to give him one more chance.

Several weeks later, on my way to the Greyhound, I saw Patty standing on the corner of Turk and Taylor Streets. She was wearing a low-cut blouse, a micro mini-skirt, black fishnet stockings, and a pair of spiked high-heeled shoes. This corner was a popular spot for local prostitutes. How sad. It was hard to believe this was the same fresh-faced girl from New Hampshire I had seen in my office a number of months back. Patty didn't see me, and I didn't try to talk to her—I knew there was nothing I could say or do at this point that would make any difference.

Another month went by. Then one afternoon I received a call from Patty. She was in the county jail and asked if I would visit. When I saw her the next day she told me what happened. Her boyfriend had robbed a Japanese tourist that she was "with" in a Tenderloin hotel room. The tourist had shocked them both by running stark naked out of the room, out of the hotel, and out onto the street. A police officer happened to be walking by—Patty and her boyfriend were immediately arrested.

Patty was ashamed of herself and determined to get her life together—no more drugs, no more prostitution, no more boyfriend. She would move out of the Tenderloin to another part of the city. But there was a problem. She'd heard that municipal judges were usually lenient with prostitutes, but she was also up for armed robbery. She asked if I would write a letter to the court on her behalf.

I sat there for a moment considering her request. Was she serious about turning her life around? I wasn't so sure, but I knew that with a break from the judge she would get out of jail long before her boyfriend. Away from his direct influence, *maybe* she really would move on with her life. This might be her big chance; it might be her only chance.

I decided to write the letter. I described Patty's arrival in San Francisco and her serious efforts to find work. I documented her contacts with me and the downward spiral of events after getting involved with the boyfriend. While acknowledging she was responsible for her actions, I asked the court to give her an opportunity to get on with her life. My statement must have helped. Because it was her first offense, she served only two weeks and was put on probation. Her boyfriend, on the other hand, was sentenced to a year in state prison.

Patty came to see me at the Greyhound after her release. The good news was that she was staying with people in the Mission district and had signed up for work at several temp agencies; the bad news was that she'd received a letter from her boyfriend promising that things would be different when he was released. She said people can change—if he really had a new attitude, maybe things could work out.

It was disheartening to have to remind her that the man she was *still* calling her "boyfriend" was an opportunistic hustler who had been manipulating her from the start. I told her that this was her opportunity to escape—to continue on with him would only be courting further disaster. I did everything I could to let her know she deserved a better life.

But it was clear she'd made up her mind to wait for him. As we stood there in the Greyhound, there was nothing left to say. Patty thanked me for all my help, said good-bye, and walked out of the bus station. I never saw her again.

I have no idea what happened to Patty. But as she left the depot that day, I recalled a prior Travelers Aid case. A Tenderloin prostitute, emotionally battered and all used up, had been dumped off at our Travelers Aid booth by her heartless pimp. "Get her out of here!" was all he said before turning his back and walking away. Would this be Patty's fate too? After she was all used up, would her pimp "boyfriend" also dump her at the Greyhound? Would Travelers Aid have to help her return to New Hampshire just as we'd helped this other woman return home? Hopefully, Patty changed her mind and never got back with her "boyfriend." Hopefully, she was able to move on with her life. Hopefully.

The Tenderloin was filled with young women like Patty who traveled out to San Francisco with high hopes but lost their way. And while Patty was apparently not ready to leave her situation, Laura couldn't wait to get away from hers.

The Steel Executive's Daughter

...deliver us from evil...
—Matthew 6:13

I first saw Laura at our office on Mason Street. In her late twenties, she had long brown hair and was wearing a purple cotton dress. She had the look of a former cheerleader who had seen better days. She was living with "some junkies" in the Tenderloin and desperately needed to get away from them. Without elaborating, she said things had deteriorated in the household and she felt her life was in danger. She was being watched wherever she went. Unable to go to the police because the situation was "too complex," she hoped Travelers Aid could assist her in leaving the city. When asked about possible resources, she mentioned her father was a wealthy steel executive, but that she was estranged from him and most of her family.

Her Tenderloin household had sent her to Travelers Aid to get food for everyone. With her upper class background, she'd been tapped as the one most likely to "score" a food voucher with "agency types." But just because they thought she was suited for the job didn't mean they trusted her—one of her housemates had accompanied her and he was waiting downstairs. She said that on one level she had come to Travelers Aid for the group, but on a personal level she had come for herself. She needed help devising an escape plan to leave both the group *and* the city—and she needed to enact the plan quickly.

Technically, Laura wasn't eligible for Travelers Aid because she'd been living in San Francisco more than forty-five days. But given her circumstances, it seemed important to try and help her.

However, to assist her responsibly we needed to confirm she had a definite place to stay somewhere.

As we explored possible resources, she remembered an aunt in Pasadena who might take her in. They had once been close and so, hoping for the best, Laura gave her a call. Not going into detail, she told her aunt she was in danger and needed to leave San Francisco as soon as possible. Without any hesitation the aunt told Laura she could come and stay with her—she would even prepay Laura's airline ticket.

When I got on the phone with the aunt, we agreed she would buy a plane ticket for that coming Saturday and then call me with the necessary flight information. Now that we had an "escape plan," I gave Laura a food voucher for her household and told her to come back in two days for another one. This supplemental voucher would give Laura a legitimate reason to return to our office to learn the flight details I'd be getting from her aunt without making her roommates suspicious.

Her aunt called several hours later with the flight information—Laura's plane was scheduled to leave San Francisco at one o'clock Saturday afternoon and her ticket would be waiting at the airline ticket counter. Her aunt would meet her when she arrived in Los Angeles.

Two days later, Laura came by the Mason Street office for the second food voucher. Once again, a roommate accompanied her and was waiting downstairs. I gave Laura the voucher along with the flight details. Everything was set for Saturday. To give her a valid reason for coming to the Greyhound, she would tell her household that Travelers Aid was providing them with one final food voucher on Saturday morning at ten o'clock. If they wondered why she was picking the voucher up at the depot, she would let them know our main office was closed on the weekend. But as soon as she arrived at the depot, I would give her a bus ticket to the airport. If someone in her household tried to intervene, I would call Greyhound security.

On Saturday morning I alerted security regarding Laura's situation. They were ready in case of trouble, but there was to be no incident. When Laura showed up at the bus station, she was alone and smiling—her housemates had been up late partying the night before and were still in bed when she left. She'd taken advantage of the situation and packed a small bag with some of her things.

I handed Laura her bus ticket and walked her out to the departure gate—her roommates nowhere in sight. Thanking Travelers Aid, she stepped into the bus and was soon headed down Mission Street on her way to the airport. Other than the drug scene she alluded to, I never really knew what was going on in her life. But it didn't matter. Thanks to her aunt in Pasadena, Laura was being given a new lease on life.

Like so many people trapped in the inner city, Laura had to *leave* the Tenderloin to get her life together. Ironically, Robert Simms had to *come* to the Tenderloin to get his life together.

Robert and the Tenderloin Guide

Two are better than one; because they
have a good reward for their labour.

—Ecclesiastes 4:9

A wonderful aroma floated through the KGO-TV studio. Earlier in the televised program a gourmet chef had prepared an early morning treat for San Francisco viewers. Off camera, San Francisco Examiner film critic Stanley Eichelbaum had already finished his review of a recent movie. On camera, Mark Murphy, a local jazz singer, was in the middle of a song. In less than five minutes, Robert Simms and I would be sitting in front of Channel 7's live TV cameras being interviewed by popular talk show host Sonny Buxton on his program AM San Francisco. We'd been invited on the program to discuss our recently published Tenderloin survival guide, *Living on Little or Nothing in Downtown San Francisco.*

After Mark Murphy finished his song and the commercial was winding down, I realized we would be on the air in just a moment or two. The thought of all those Bay Area viewers watching us was almost paralyzing. As a studio technician led us onto the set and clipped little microphones on our shirts, I turned to Robert and asked if he was nervous. "No way," he said smiling, "I always wanted to be on TV. This is fun." Still grinning, he looked at me reassuringly. "Relax; we're going to be great."

As we sat there together, I marveled at the irony of our situation and the unique circumstances that had brought us into the TV studio. For the last five months I had been Robert's Travelers Aid social worker, encouraging and supporting him in a variety of ways. Now here he was encouraging and supporting me.

Suddenly lights flashed, cameras moved in, and we were on the air. Host Sonny Buxton described our Tenderloin survival guide in glowing terms to his audience. As he did, I began to relax ever so slightly. And as I watched our images on the monitor, I felt a deep appreciation for the special relationship Robert and I had developed over the past number of months. He'd come to Travelers Aid in serious trouble, and I'd seen him regularly as he struggled to get his life back on track. A mutual respect had emerged and an inner-city guidebook was born from our work together.

So here we were, social worker and client, co-authors and friends, on television sharing our amazing adventure. The TV program was the culmination of the improbable events that had brought two strangers together to produce not only an inner-city survival guide, but also a most unconventional friendship.

Robert came to Travelers Aid for assistance when he was on the streets and truly desperate—he had no money, no food, and no shelter. Carol first saw him in the main office. She housed him at the Coronado and then transferred his case to me because we agreed that, as the nighttime social worker, I would be in the best position to provide him with ongoing support.

Robert was polite and soft-spoken. He came from a black, upper middle-class family on the East Coast. College educated and extremely bright, he wore glasses and was of medium height. Even with his recent troubles, he retained his quirky sense of humor. When I asked him in our first meeting what he thought of San Francisco, he said that so far it hadn't exactly been "a Tony Bennett, little-cable-cars-climbing-to-the-stars kind of experience." He then led me through the series of events that culminated in his recent homelessness and depression.

Robert had been working for a large health organization in Washington, D.C. The job looked good on paper, but he grew bored. Drinking excessively and living extravagantly, he was waking up in Hilton Hotel rooms he didn't remember checking into. He started piling up huge debt on his credit cards and eventually exhausted his savings. With mounting bills and great feelings of guilt, he quit his job and took a Greyhound bus to San Francisco. "From the

Hilton to the hound" was the way Robert put it, always trying to inject some humor into his desperate situation.

But as soon as he arrived in San Francisco, he resumed his lavish lifestyle. Staying at the Mark Hopkins Hotel on posh Nob Hill, he spent what was left on his credit cards. Suddenly he found himself homeless—and now there were no more credit cards and no more games to play. Aimlessly walking the streets, he became seriously depressed and was eventually hospitalized at San Francisco General Hospital—but was quickly discharged and once again on the streets. That's when he called Travelers Aid for help. Our number was listed on a resource sheet he'd been given when he left the hospital.

During our first meeting, we worked out a survival plan that would keep him temporarily housed at the Coronado Hotel. I also went over the community resources he would need to start using when he had to leave the hotel. These included all the missions, crash pads, free meal programs, and employment services that were available at the time. While he would soon be on his own, I would remain available for emotional support. Robert was adamant that he didn't want to apply for aid at the San Francisco Department of Social Services. He said he could handle the "survival stuff"— but welcomed the personal support. We agreed to meet again the following week.

Robert was motivated and resourceful and more than met the challenge of surviving in the inner city. After he left the Coronado, he began staying in local missions as he looked for employment. He found day-work tossing handbills on people's front porches in various neighborhoods around the city. He also picked up periodic cash giving blood at the plasma center on Mission Street, all the while checking out job leads at places like the Tenderloin Employment Office. I informed him that Time-Life Books was always looking for part-time telephone sales people, and that I liked working there when I was fairly new to the city.

To my surprise, Robert *enjoyed* the day-to-day challenge of trying to survive in the inner city. He would become very animated as he described the ins-and-outs of throwing handbills, eating lunch at St. Anthony's, or staying at one of the missions.

During one of our impromptu meetings, I asked if he thought he was ready for a job out there in the nine-to-five world. He laughed a bit nervously and said "probably not." He was surprised when I agreed with his assessment and suggested that, at least for the time being, he should drop the idea of looking for full-time work. He was becoming a survival expert and was learning a lot about himself in the process. He seemed so happy doing what he was doing. We agreed he should re-enter the world on his own terms— not society's, our agency's, or anyone else's.

"I can't explain it," Robert remarked somewhat quizzically, "but every day I'm so excited just to wake up to the challenge of another day. I have no idea where I am going to sleep that night or what I might learn that will be helpful to me or to someone else. My life is anything but boring or routine. It's an incredible adventure that requires a certain resourcefulness I didn't know I had. More than anything, I have a desire to help others in the Tenderloin who aren't aware of what's available to them. It may sound weird, but being on the streets has opened me up in a way I could have never imagined. For the first time ever, I feel totally alive."

As the weeks went by, I saw Robert regularly. I knew through the grapevine that he'd gained the respect of many street people for his knowledge of inner-city resources. One night, as we ate at the budget-priced Communion Restaurant on Folsom Street near the Greyhound, I asked how things were going. He said his life on the streets was still very meaningful. He was meeting people he would have never encountered in the regular work world, and he was helping others by sharing what he had learned. We both noted the irony of what was happening—Robert was pulling his life together in a San Francisco neighborhood where many people's lives were falling apart. What he was doing made sense for him and his life was reflecting that.

As we continued to meet each week, Robert would describe the new resources he'd discovered and the people he'd met and assisted. He was seeing everything from a street level perspective. Some days he would arrive early for the free lunch at St. Anthony's just to share his knowledge of community resources with those around him. In the middle of the Tenderloin and in his own way, Robert was making peace with himself.

Then one night Robert told me he'd taken a part-time job with Time-Life Books. He said he wasn't ready for full-time employment yet, but this part-time position seemed like a good place to begin. He still enjoyed the streets, but felt his life was changing in subtle ways. After his first paycheck, he rented a weekly room at the Empress, an inexpensive Tenderloin hotel much like the Coronado.

One afternoon as we talked in the main office, Robert told me about a small bakery he had discovered in the Tenderloin— the Adeline Bake Shop—that sold day-old donuts for a dime and offered free refills on their twenty-five cent coffee. Listening to him talk about the bakery, I thought of the incredible knowledge we'd both accumulated about the inner city. Not just the obvious stuff, but places even many locals would never know, like the Adeline Bake Shop at Sixth and Mission. Or, the budget priced Fantastic Foods Restaurant at Seventh and Market where friendly Chinese owner Andrew Huang cooked New Orleans style red beans and rice along with his usual chow mein and chop suey. And while I knew a lot about local resources, Robert was the one who had lived, breathed, and actually experienced everything. He'd slept in the shelters and missions and knew which ones were the cleanest, friendliest, and had the most comfortable beds. He knew where to get food, which medical clinics and job counselors *really* cared about street people, and even where you could go to shoot a free game of pool. Suddenly it hit me.

"Robert, with what you and I know about the Tenderloin, we should write a survival guide." As soon as I said it, we both knew we were going to do it. I picked up the phone and called a Travelers Aid board member who was on the Community Action Team at Levi Strauss & Co. and told her about our idea for a Tenderloin survival guide. She thought it was a great idea and advised us to submit a proposal. A week later, Levi Strauss approved our request and provided funding for the guide. We were on our way.

For Robert, the guide became yet one more challenge. For the next several months, he and I worked our way through the roughly forty-three square-block area of San Francisco known as the Tenderloin/Central City. We visited every hotel, restaurant, medical clinic, social service agency, counseling service, employment service, church office, senior center, veterans group, prisoner outreach, rescue mission, thrift shop, blood bank, day-labor office, cut-rate movie theater, and pool hall. If it was in the Tenderloin area, we checked it out, and we listed everything we thought would be helpful. Working on the guide became the backbone of our time together. The line between Travelers Aid social worker and Travelers Aid client became indistinguishable as we collaborated on the project.

About two months into our work on the guide, Robert told me he had taken a full-time position at a local bank. I wasn't surprised because I'd seen him slowly but surely working his way back into the day-to-day work world he'd so completely abandoned when he left Washington, D.C. He also had a girlfriend with whom he was spending a lot of time—but even with these changes he still kept working with me on the guide.

When we finished our research, the job of compiling all the information began. We decided to call our survival guide *Living on Little or Nothing in Downtown San Francisco: A Guide to the Tenderloin/Central City Area*. We spent night after night refining the guide. We enjoyed the creative process of editing and putting all our listings into an imaginative yet easy-to-read format. We marveled at how well we worked together. When one of us ran out of words or ideas, the other seemed to step in with what was needed. We took great pride in what we were doing and knew the guide would help many people.

Finally the day came when we hit the streets with the first printing of our Tenderloin guide. It was free and the demand was instant and heavy. The *San Francisco Chronicle* ran a full-page story about the guide and my Travelers Aid job at the Greyhound bus station; Robert's involvement with the project was featured in his bank's monthly newsletter. *Living on Little or Nothing in Downtown San Francisco* was being regarded as an important resource for inner-city people and Robert and I were like proud fathers. Then amidst all of the excitement came the invitation to appear on Channel 7's *AM San Francisco*.

On the program, Robert looked so dapper in his suit and tie that he was the one introduced as the Travelers Aid social worker. Because I was wearing my usual jeans and hiking boots, I was introduced as the former Tenderloin street person. After straightening out this initial confusion, Robert and I talked about the survival guide and then took questions from viewers. Our segment on the show went well—and then suddenly it was over. The lights went off, the microphones were removed from our shirts, we shook hands with the host, and walked out of the studio and onto the street.

In a Tenderloin pub we drank sodas, shot pool, critiqued the program, and reflected on our time together over the past five months. What an adventure it had been! For Robert it had been a journey from the streets of the Tenderloin to Channel 7 television—from being unemployed to co-authoring a survival guide and getting a full-time job at a local bank. He had been an inspiration to me and to so many other people in the Tenderloin.

When there was nothing more to say, we sat quietly as the finality of the moment hit home. We knew this season in our lives was ending. His regular meetings with me, working on the guide, and all the media aftermath were over. After spending so much time together, we would now be heading in different directions. I told him how much fun I'd had and how proud I was of him. It was a happy but bittersweet moment as we parted. We had a great feeling of accomplishment, but we both knew it was time to move on.

Robert was well on his way to a more stable life. He received a quick promotion at his bank and would soon be married. As for me, the next summer I would leave San Francisco to take a social work job in a rural Northern California community. And while our lives took divergent paths, neither of us would ever forget the extraordinary time we had writing a guidebook about living on little or nothing in downtown San Francisco.

Just as my Travelers Aid client became my friend, so did the reporter who wrote about our survival guide in the *San Francisco Chronicle*. His name was Joseph Torchia.

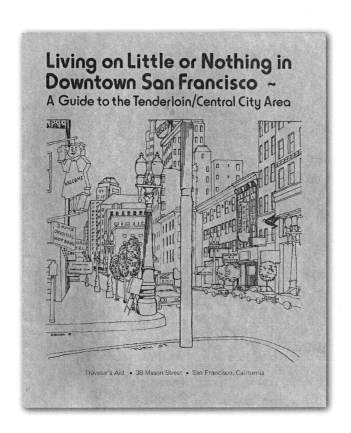

Living on Little or Nothing in Downtown San Francisco ~
A Guide to the Tenderloin/Central City Area

WELCOME

SAM'S
ORIGINAL
HOFBRAU

TURK ST

Traveler's Aid • 38 Mason Street • San Francisco, California

The Travelers Aid Survival Guide

The Chronicle Reporter

...and plead the cause of the poor and needy.

—Proverbs 31:9

The *San Francisco Chronicle* newspaper had been alerted to our survival guide and my Travelers Aid job at the bus station. Joseph Torchia, a feature writer for the paper, called and made an appointment to interview me. He also wanted to accompany me on my night rounds as I worked on the streets and down at the depot.

I liked Joseph at once. Wearing jeans, a flannel shirt, and hiking boots, he came dressed for the Tenderloin. He was in his early thirties and had thick, neatly groomed brown hair. His regularly featured articles in the "People" section of the *Chronicle* had a distinctive personal touch that was both unique and endearing. For an interview with *Hello Dolly* actress Carol Channing, for instance, he took her tea dancing at the Hyatt-Regency Hotel, and his story was based almost completely on his personal interaction with her that evening. It was a great article. Whether he was in his tux with Carol Channing at the Hyatt-Regency or in his jeans with me in the Tenderloin, Joseph immersed himself in his subject and gave it his all.

During the interview in our main office, I gave him an overview of Travelers Aid and our various outreach services. After recounting several unusual cases, I described some of the more day-to-day situations we encountered—a Cuban couple trying to relocate from Miami; a young man trying to get to San Jose to join the carnival; a medical student from England who had arrived ahead of his funds; a Belgian tourist robbed in Berkeley;

the woman who had a heart attack on a bus to Los Angeles; the man whose flight was canceled due to flooding in Boston; and a family fleeing the recent violence in their Detroit neighborhood. There was the Polish floral peddler from Buffalo, the portly potato farmer from Idaho, and the itinerant cook from Medicine Bend, Wyoming—all needing assistance for one reason or another at the Greyhound bus station. I told Joseph I could go on and on describing the parade of people and problems we saw every day in our main office and down at the depot.

When I'd finished explaining what Travelers Aid was all about, we headed out into the Tenderloin. For many years the Tenderloin was the official red-light district in the city, but in 1923 prostitution was legally outlawed. Three hundred angry prostitutes protested the ban by picketing the house of the minister responsible for the new law. Since then, the Tenderloin has been the *unofficial* red-light district of San Francisco. Without betraying any confidentiality, I told Joseph about several of the young women we had seen at Travelers Aid—how they'd come to San Francisco looking for legitimate work, only to end up as prostitutes in the Tenderloin.

Joseph witnessed an especially busy evening as he accompanied me on my rounds. Ducking in and out of phone booths, I fielded countless calls when paged from our switchboard. As we dashed around the Tenderloin, I showed him the Coronado Hotel, the Tenderloin Clinic, St. Anthony's Dining Hall, and a number of the other key organizations that worked with us. I pointed out Newman's Gym on Leavenworth Street, where legendary boxers Jack Dempsey and George Foreman once trained. On the edge of the Tenderloin on O'Farrell Street, we walked past the ACT Theater where the man dressed in a top hat, white tie, and tails regularly entertained playgoers. As usual, he was playing piano in the back of his pickup truck that was conveniently parked in front of the theater. His tip jar was filled to the brim.

Later, when we arrived at the Greyhound, I was approached by a homeless family from Oklahoma that had been waiting in the lobby. The husband couldn't find work in Fresno, so they'd taken a Greyhound bus to San Francisco. After taking the family to McDonald's to eat, Joseph and I walked them up to the YMCA Hotel where they would be housed for several nights. I suggested they go to the Department of Social Services the next day to seek assistance until the husband found work. Once they were checked in, Joseph and I returned to the bus station where I worked with more people. By the end of the evening, the *Chronicle* reporter had a good feel for what Travelers Aid was doing at the Greyhound, in our main office, and on the streets of San Francisco.

At ten o'clock I signed off as usual with the answering service. They would forward any further calls to the Night Minister until our main office opened again in the morning. After I closed the booth, Joseph and I relaxed in the lobby. I answered a few last questions about my job, and then we talked more generally about our own lives.

He said he was writing a book called *The Kryptonite Kid*. It was a novel about a young boy who found comfort writing non-stop letters to Superman—even though Superman never responded. Joseph told me he was gay, and that the book was a way for him to process many of his feelings. While he enjoyed writing for the *Chronicle*, he hoped to become an independent writer one day. When he asked me about my commitment to social work, I told him it began with volunteering for Travelers Aid. Joseph found it amusing that I was involved with someone I'd met in the Greyhound lobby. He told me his best friend was his beloved cat "Ditto." Finally, as it was getting late, we said goodnight and agreed to stay in touch.

Several days later, on October 5, 1977, Joseph's full-page article about my after-hours job with Travelers Aid was featured in the "People" section of the *San Francisco Chronicle*. The headline read "Despair on the Street," and a sidebar "Surviving the Tenderloin" described our survival guide. Reading the article, I knew I would take some kidding from my co-workers when I arrived at the office. In Joseph's enthusiastic and sometimes over-the-edge writing style, he made me look like the Superman of the Tenderloin—rushing like Clark Kent into Tenderloin telephone booths to save the day. He wrote:

> There they are: The street people, the hustlers, the homeless, the jobless, the hungry, the disabled, the runaways, the battered women and defenseless elderly and walking suicides of the Tenderloin.
>
> There he is: Warren Smith, 31, walking the same night-streets, passing the same porno shops and dirty-movie houses and dark doorways, talking about the hundreds of people who pour into the Greyhound bus station on Seventh Street—who come to San Francisco "in search of better things" and end up penniless, alone, stranded and struggling to survive.
>
> "It's another world down here," Smith says matter-of-factly, as he walks the streets in his hiking boots, knapsack and Tel-Page beeper—waiting for the battery-operated BEEEEEEP that will send him rushing to the nearest phone booth to make a call that will tell him yet another man or woman or teenager or family has landed in San Francisco, is desperate for help, for money, for food, for medical attention—"for some caring."

Joseph went on to describe his evening with me in the Tenderloin and some of the people I'd recently assisted, one of them being a young man we'd helped return home to Colorado after being sexually assaulted by four men in an alley near the Greyhound depot.

Although his article focused on my after-hours job at the Greyhound, it emphasized the overall mission of Travelers Aid as an indispensable service organization in the Tenderloin. More than anything it brought the plight of inner-city people to the public's attention. Because it featured our survival guide, Travelers Aid had a flood of requests after his article. Joseph later did a series of follow-up stories on the Tenderloin, including one, the "Depot Dwellers," that took a more in-depth look at the bus station itself. In writing these and other articles, Joseph became a strong advocate for the inner-city poor. Joseph and I met together several more times over the coming months. When I moved out of the city the following summer, we stayed in contact for five or six years.

In one of my visits to the city, he told me the gay scene in San Francisco had changed dramatically; HIV/AIDS was terrifying everyone. Many of his friends and acquaintances were sick or dying. I remember the fear I saw on his face as he described the prevalence of this new disease. Perhaps he already knew that last time we met—Joseph died of complications from AIDS in 1996. The Kryptonite Kid's worst fears had come to pass.

I didn't hear about Joseph's death until a decade after the fact, but when I did I tracked down his brother to express my condolences. He said when Joseph left his job at the *San Francisco Chronicle*, he'd opened a photography studio in Napa and that his work was highly acclaimed throughout the Napa Valley region. At one point in our conversation it was hard for either one of us to speak. Joseph had been such a special person—just ask Carol Channing, or any of us who knew him, was interviewed by him, or who read his exceptional articles. I was sad to have lost touch with Joseph. But perhaps more than anything, I just felt grateful to have crossed paths with the *Chronicle* reporter who had become my friend—if only for a while.

While Joseph brought much-needed attention to the plight of those living in the Tenderloin, a Hollywood producer wanted to bring that same attention to the big screen.

The Hollywood Producer

Cast me not off in the time of old age;
forsake me not when my strength faileth.
—Psalm 71:9

A Hollywood producer had been given my name as a resource person for the Greyhound bus station and the Tenderloin. He called and asked if we could meet and discuss a movie script he was working on. We agreed to meet at the Jack-in-the-Box restaurant on the corner of Market Street across from the Greyhound.

After basic introductions, he told me the movie he was hoping to produce was about a group of low-income seniors living in the Tenderloin. Tired of being robbed, and unable to afford even cheap Tenderloin hotels, these renegade seniors hijack a Greyhound bus and drive it to the Sierra Nevada Mountains. Here they pool their Social Security checks to rent a mountain home, grow their own food, and live communally. With an affordable place in a beautiful area, they are now able to live more economically and with dignity. This rag-tag bunch of Tenderloin seniors—sort of a Tenderloin "Over the Hill Gang"—forge new relationships with each other and their neighbors in their greatly improved rural living environment.

The movie was to be a direct indictment of the escalating prices and appalling conditions many seniors were forced to endure in cities like Los Angeles and San Francisco. The Hollywood producer hoped the seniors' unorthodox (albeit illegal) solution to their predicament—commandeering a Greyhound bus and moving to the mountains—would help stimulate more meaningful discussion about poor urban seniors who are forced to live in unsafe areas like the Tenderloin.

We had an animated discussion for over an hour discussing the Tenderloin. I described some of the seniors I met and worked with at the Greyhound and on the streets. I was glad to share whatever information might be helpful to his project. It was encouraging to know that someone from Hollywood was taking an interest in the struggles of inner-city seniors.

As part of his series on the Tenderloin, my new friend, *San Francisco Chronicle* reporter Joseph Torchia, had written an article about some of the people who hang out at the Greyhound bus station. In his November 8, 1977 story entitled the "Depot Dwellers," he featured a Tenderloin senior who was one of our Greyhound "regulars." Ninety-one year-old Teddy, for lack of money and anything better to do, spent as much as six hours a day sitting in the Greyhound lobby. He regarded the Greyhound as his second home and was a familiar fixture to us all. In writing about Teddy, Joseph perfectly described the type of senior the producer was picturing for his proposed movie:

> His name is Teddy and he sits on an end seat, his head slumped over his chest, his back to a cigarette machine, his white hands scratching his unshaven face and his 91 years of wrinkles.
>
> He comes to the bus station about six hours a day, always taking a different seat, always trying to dissolve into the surroundings, always reading his newspaper and keeping an eye out for the security guard, who might ask him to leave—and admitting that he wouldn't be surprised if he dropped dead right here, right now, in this seat, in this bus station, just a block from the sleazy hotel he's trying to escape.
>
> "I got bad knees, bad eyes, bad hearing, no teeth and nowhere else to go," he says—with no bitterness, with no regret—just another fact of life.
>
> "This place is as good as any," Teddy says. "You can't be in your room 24 hours a day—not when you ain't got no TV, no radio, no stove, no room to move around . . ."

Teddy was indeed one of the many seniors trapped in the inner city, living in a cheap hotel, just trying to keep his head above water. He would carefully weave his way along the city streets, avoiding eye contact with other people, hoping not to be robbed on his way to the store, or the doctor, or the bus station. There were countless other Tenderloin seniors who felt trapped in their apartments or drab hotel rooms. More than a few of them would come to the Greyhound to be around other people and to pass the time of day. Some fortunate seniors, like Willis Potter, made it out of the Tenderloin to safer neighborhoods. Others, like Teddy, were stuck right where they were.

If the Hollywood producer's film ever made it to theaters or television, I never knew it. But had that producer come back to San Francisco with a casting director, I would have led him right over to Teddy or one of the many other Tenderloin seniors who made the Greyhound their second home. In no time flat they would have their amazing "Over the Hill Gang." In fact, our Greyhound regulars would probably have been only too glad to commandeer a Greyhound bus and make the Sierra Nevada Mountains their new home. Until then, Teddy and all the other forgotten Tenderloin seniors would have to wait for a better day.

And while seniors like Teddy were forced to remain in the Tenderloin, I was forced out of the Tenderloin. When funding for my Travelers Aid position at the Greyhound unexpectedly disappeared, I didn't just leave my job—I left San Francisco.

Travelers Aid and Greyhound Again

That which hath been is now; and that
which is to be hath already been...

—Ecclesiastes 3:15

In the months after the publication of the Tenderloin guide, the *San Francisco Chronicle* article, and meeting with the Hollywood producer, my time with Travelers Aid quickly wound down. In the spring, a primary funding source vanished overnight, and money for the after-hours program was gone. I was given two weeks' notice and would have to find another job.

My final days were filled with the usual challenges of helping our clients—then it was over. No more nights at the Greyhound. No more travelers in trouble. Now I was the one who had to figure out what to do next.

On my last day at work, the office staff took me to Tu Lan, a neighborhood Vietnamese restaurant Robert and I had listed in our Tenderloin guide. We sat at a long table and reflected on our time together. I would miss this dedicated group of people who had been so supportive and great to work with—especially Arlin, Cate, Carol, Ginny, and Debbie. After the meal and fond farewells at the office, I headed down to the Greyhound for my final night at the depot.

In the course of the evening, I saw the usual mix of tourists asking for directions and clients asking for help. As I closed up the Travelers Aid booth at the end of the night, I stood for a moment looking around the lobby. Flashing back on all that had transpired over the past two years, I knew I had seen just about everything. Later, after saying good-bye to our Travelers

Aid volunteer and the Greyhound staff, I walked out of the bus station for the last time. It was hard to believe it was over.

My girlfriend Kari helped me find my next job. Several weeks after leaving Travelers Aid, she took me over to the employment office at the University of California at Berkeley where she was finishing her degree. There on the bulletin board was an announcement for a social work position in a Northern California town three-and-a-half hours from San Francisco. Kari and I didn't know it at the time, but the job would lead me not only out of San Francisco, but ultimately out of her life—and it would be in this new town that I would meet Joy—the woman who would eventually become my wife.

The day before I left for my new hometown, I asked a U-Haul dealer to attach one of their trailers to the back of the Toyota pickup truck I'd purchased after abandoning my VW in New Mexico. The next morning, after loading my things into the U-Haul, I set out for my new home.

After driving up Highway 101, north of the Golden Gate Bridge, I cut over to Highway 37 and drove east through the open valley. After descending a steep bridge in Vallejo, I noticed the U-Haul trailer seemed to be weaving a bit from side to side. When I gently applied my brakes, the trailer completely separated from the back of the truck. As the trailer raced by me in the passing lane to my left, I watched in disbelief as the U-Haul—with all my belongings—crossed over the median to the other side of the highway. The detached trailer, not missing a beat, was now speeding down the opposite lane against traffic. Nearly colliding with a huge truck that was in its path, the trailer suddenly veered to the left and came to a stop along the edge of the pavement.

I pulled off to the side of the road and jumped out of my truck. Making my way across the highway, I rushed over to the U-Haul. Stunned by what had just happened, it took all my strength to push the trailer completely off the road. I badly strained my neck in the process. I then went back across the highway and walked up a hill to an office building where I called U-Haul.

The company sent a driver over right away. When he arrived, he agreed that U-Haul was responsible for the poor hook-up. Seeing my frazzled state, the sympathetic worker attached the wayward trailer to his company truck and followed me all the way to my new home. I didn't miss the irony of needing some "travelers aid" to get me to my destination.

I spent the next day unpacking and getting settled in my new house. At nightfall, I sat on my enclosed back porch and looked out the window. I thought my eyes had to be deceiving me. Across the way, slightly above the neighbor's rooftop in front of me, was a familiar sign silhouetted against the evening sky. I couldn't believe it—I was living only a block away from the local Greyhound bus station! Wherever I was now headed in my life, the Greyhound was there to remind me of where I had already been.

The next part of my story continues in another book— *The Light That Was Dark*—but this part of my story ends here. Travelers Aid had done for me what it tries to do for all the people it serves: It enabled me to move on with my life.

Being a Travelers Aid volunteer at the Greyhound had opened up a whole new world to me. As a result, I was inspired to make social work my life's work. After graduate school, Travelers Aid gave me my first social work job—and what a job it was! I will be forever grateful for all of those amazing days and nights with Travelers Aid in the heart—yes, the heart—of San Francisco.

Vintage photo of the former San Francisco Greyhound Bus Terminal
(Photo from the History Center, San Francisco Public Library)

Epilogue

Most of San Francisco was destroyed in the 1906 earthquake and fire. Hardly any of the city's landmark buildings survived. The Old Mint and the Main Post Office were among the few. However, many structures built after the earthquake still stand today and serve as testimony to the city's "can do" spirit in the face of tragedy and despair.

San Francisco, by virtue of its own history, is extremely sympathetic to those who are trying to move on with their lives. After the 1906 earthquake, over 500 city blocks (four square miles) were burned to the ground. More than 250,000 San Franciscans were suddenly stranded and homeless. Tent cities were erected in city parks and countless numbers of San Franciscans were fed daily at long tables set up downtown in Union Square. Housing and feeding the homeless is part of the city's history and legacy. In 1914, eight years after the earthquake, Travelers Aid became part of that legacy.

Local religious organizations have also been an important part of that same caring history. Many of the churches Travelers Aid worked with continue to serve the homeless and needy in their original Tenderloin locations. For example, St. Boniface Church still feeds the homeless at St. Anthony's Dining Room at 45 Jones Street. Glide Memorial Church provides its numerous ongoing services at 333 Ellis Street. The San Francisco Gospel Mission continues to serve the homeless at 219 Sixth Street and Raphael House still serves homeless families at 1065 Sutter.

Many of the hotels that Travelers Aid worked with in the Tenderloin also stand in their original locations. The Coronado Hotel remains at 373 Ellis Street; the Arlington is at 480 Ellis Street; and the YMCA Hotel is at 220 Golden Gate Avenue. Other hotels such as the Windsor, the Ambassador, and the Empress also remain in their original locations.

But while many Tenderloin buildings, churches, hotels, and restaurants have survived the march of time, the Greyhound Bus Terminal did not. Where the busy depot once stood at Seventh and Mission, an eighteen-story federal office building stands in its place. No longer having its own exclusive terminal, Greyhound Bus Lines now operates out of the downtown Transbay Terminal. And while our former office building at 38 Mason Street still remains, Travelers Aid itself is gone. Many of its functions have been absorbed by other agencies, but Travelers Aid's unique presence in the Tenderloin and in the city of San Francisco is no longer there.

Travelers Aid and the Greyhound depot may have disappeared from the city, but my memories of those days remain vivid and clear. Sometimes late at night, even after all these years, I can still hear the hum of those Greyhound buses like it was yesterday. I see Banjo Bobby Brown parading around the Greyhound lobby, and Willis Potter sitting in that same Greyhound lobby waiting to die. I hear the Bluesman playing his guitar and inspiring that wonderful Greyhound sing-a-long. I remember Lenny and Ronnie boarding their bus to freedom with Ronnie smiling and shouting, "Hey Warren, no more fat nurse!" I recall the Thompson family heading back to Tennessee with their "heap of change," and Robert Simms and I writing our survival guide and appearing on television together. I see Tyrone smiling in front of the Bank of America, Renee sketching my caricature, the Oklahoma Kid playing pinball amidst all the Greyhound regulars, Lily's elation after visiting her nephew at San Quentin, the Dalton's marriage ceremony with me as the best man, "Amazing Grace" about to gain her sight, and Waldo Weinstein's simple wish to have a girlfriend like mine—only Jewish, and in his size.

What a joy and privilege it was to work for Travelers Aid and to have been a part of San Francisco's utterly unique Tenderloin neighborhood. I have had some great jobs in social work, but there has never been anything quite like that incredible time of watering the Greyhound garden.

> *And the Lord shall guide thee continually,*
> *and satisfy thy soul in drought...*
> *and thou shalt be like a watered garden...*
> —Isaiah 58:11